"In *The Courage to Trust,* Cynthia Wall helps us to discover the genuine source of much of our pain and the pain in our relationships and offers us simple, powerful ways to begin to heal it. This wise and beautifully written book is a blessing for every friend, every parent, every lover and every human being."

—Rachel Naomi Remen, MD, clinical professor of family and community medicine at the University of California, San Francisco, School of Medicine; medical director of the Commonweal Cancer Help Program; and author of *Kitchen Table Wisdom* and *My Grandfather's Blessings*

the courage to trust

A Guide
to Building
Deep and
Lasting
Relationships

CYNTHIA L. WALL, LCSW

New Harbinger Publications, Inc.

Publisher's Note

This publication is designed to provide accurate and authoritative information in regard to the subject matter covered. It is sold with the understanding that the publisher is not engaged in rendering psychological, financial, legal, or other professional services. If expert assistance or counseling is needed, the services of a competent professional should be sought.

Copyright © 2004 by Cynthia Wall
New Harbinger Publications, Inc.
5674 Shattuck Avenue
Oakland, CA 94609

The excerpt from Emily Leider's "Friends No More" was reprinted with permission from the author.

Sascha Wagner's poem was reprinted with permission from Alice J. Wisler/LARGO newsletter.

Cover design by Amy Shoup
Acquired by Melissa Kirk
Edited by Brady Kahn
Text design by Tracy Marie Carlson

ISBN-13 978-1-57224-380-4
ISBN-10 1-57224-380-5

Distributed in Canada by Raincoast Books
Printed in the United States of America

New Harbinger Publications' website address: www.newharbinger.com

16   15   14

20   19   18   17   16   15

Contents

Foreword

The ability to trust provides the bedrock for emotional security and peace of mind. Being trustworthy is the foundation of personal integrity. Why is such an essential quality often so difficult to find and so easy to lose? Thankfully, within the pages of *The Courage to Trust*, author Cynthia Wall gives readers sound answers to that question. She also provides countless tools to help you embrace trust and strengthen your ability to be trustworthy.

As a psychotherapist in private practice for over twenty-five years, I have worked with many clients who needed to establish or reestablish a sense of trust within themselves and in their lives in general. Many had been severely wounded by abuse, betrayal, and loss. However, even when spared such soul-searing experiences, many of us—myself included—still find ourselves growing into adulthood with only a tenuous and intermittent grasp on trust. Why is that?

Trust is hard to come by because it is both *learned* and *earned*. As children, we are given mixed messages that confuse us. For instance, we're expected to automatically trust people such as our parents, but they can let us down and even lie to us. When a child senses her mom is upset, asks what's wrong, and is told, "Nothing!!! Now leave me alone . . ." she will learn to doubt her own perceptions. She may also begin to believe something is wrong with her and that her feelings are flawed. As kids, we simply don't have the emotional or intellectual experience to say, "Ah ha! Mother is not telling the truth right now in hopes of sparing me the pain of knowing she's not happy today!" Because a child's safety and security depend on the big people in their lives, it's natural for them to trust adult perceptions over their own. And so begins the habit of mistrusting ourselves.

As a mother of four adult children, I have a long list of things I wish I'd done differently and actually could do differently were I parenting now that I'm older and more experienced. I did the best I could at the time and, looking back, know that my best was sometimes lousy. Because of my own regrets and those shared by clients, I sincerely believe that most parents love and care for their children to the best of their abilities a vast majority of the time. Nonetheless, we're all human and, out of ignorance and fear, we all make mistakes. One result of our own and others' mistakes is learning not to trust anyone, neither ourselves nor others.

Without trust, life is scary. Behind every experience lurks the fear of crisis, chaos, and calamity. How can we transform fear or act in spite of it? For me, the best way to keep fear from becoming a debilitating force in my life is to believe that I can survive whatever comes my way, learn from it, and move on to greater awareness. Believe me, there are times when I still run from fear, doubt myself, and assign blame to others rather than accepting responsibility. But many, many years of *choosing* to learn to trust—especially the art of self-trust—and consciously moving back into my heart, where trust resides, allows me to tame fear, regain equilibrium, and once again feel safe, secure, and confident.

Contrary to what you may believe, first and foremost, it is essential to learn to trust your self. From the deep commitment not to betray, belittle, or undermine yourself—or if you do, move back to self-love and care immediately—can flow the certainty that there is one person you can always count on—yourself. That certainty will strip power from many of your fears. Knowing you are your own best friend and greatest emotional support helps you face the vicissitudes of life with aplomb and exuberantly embrace joy when it sings in your heart. However, you only have the power to assure your *own* trustworthiness. Everyone else is in charge of his or her trustworthiness.

Because of our own emotional wounds, fears, and limiting or erroneous beliefs, we may be in the habit of trusting others unwisely or without thought. On the other hand, due to conscious or unconscious vulnerabilities and past betrayals, we may barricade our hearts and refuse to trust anyone no matter how trustworthy they may actually be. Neither pattern of behavior brings peace of mind nor solace of heart. Each sets us up for loneliness. Many of the exercises in *The Courage to Trust* are designed to help you uncover and heal the emotional triggers that impel you to trust impulsively or withhold trust altogether. Cynthia helps you learn self-trust and offers many ways in which you can allow others to earn your trust in them.

Trust in ourselves and others gives us the courage and capability to create meaningful and lasting relationships. Over time, significant relationships will encompass devotion and disappointment, support and abandonment, joy and grief. Becoming a trustworthy friend to ourselves helps us choose relationships that are right for us and weather the times when even right relationships feel wrong. Being able to trust ourselves completely makes us better friends, lovers, parents, and acquaintances. I believe that we have a deep and holy hunger for sacred partnership in close relationships. Mutual trust must exist between participants in order for any relationship to become a sacred, cherished partnership.

All of us will occasionally hurt or be hurt by others. Yes, we will experience loss again and again. No, we will not handle every encounter or experience with grace, confidence, and compassion. Yes, there will be times when we succumb to feeling overwhelmed. No, not all people are trustworthy. In spite of that, we can learn to love and trust ourselves and others. Granted, having the courage to incorporate trust into your heart takes commitment and persistence. But I truly believe if I can do it, you can too. As you move through the process of befriending trust, please remember to be gentle with yourself. Allow yourself to ask for and accept the support of friends, family, a therapist, along with this book. As with all desirable qualities, trust grows more easily in a nurturing climate than in a harsh, critical, or lonely environment.

We are bright and beautiful beings who already have everything we need within us to return to trust. By *choosing* to, you can learn to trust, know intuitively who and what has earned your trust and, therefore, trust appropriately. And the wonderful news is you don't have to do it alone. In my opinion, *The Courage to Trust* is a natural complement for both individual psychotherapy and personal growth groups. Circumstances or personality might make working alone best for you. Cynthia—a therapist herself—has provided a compassionate, insightful, and comprehensive guide to light the way. You will learn to embrace and express trust and, therefore, enhance the quality of your self-love, relationships, and life.

—Sue Patton Thoele, author of *The Courage to Be Yourself* and *Growing Hope*

Recognitions and Appreciations

I always imagined that writing a book would be a lonely process. I was wrong. It has taken many people to make this book. With the wisdom I gained in a writing class taught by Ellen Bass and by reading many books that encourage new writers, I faced the empty page with a full heart.

Sal Glynn, writing coach and book midwife, helped me understand how a book is formed. He guided me as I turned my ideas into words, the words into sentences, and the sentences into a book.

The staff at New Harbinger Publications shines at being supportive and honest. They are the lifelines a new author needs. Melissa Kirk and Catharine Sutker believed in this project and kept me moving forward. Matt McKay championed *The Courage to Trust* by lending expertise and confidence. Brady Kahn is the magician called "copyeditor" who smoothed my manuscript into a cohesive book.

Even though writing took me away from friends and family for months at a time, they all supported me with their enthusiasm for the project. Some signed on as readers, and others were willing to talk about their own experiences of trust and intimacy, which helped me express abstract ideas more authentically. Thanks to Alice Sanford, Ann Conner, Christine Samas, and Karin Gjording for your tender care.

I discovered that many of my friends were secretly writing as well. We banded together and overcame the terror of sharing our work. Friends who are experienced writers taught me how to proceed when stuck and told me that the secret incantation for success was to "just keep writing." Thanks to Kate Erickson, Annie Raitt, Christy Wagner, Theresa Whitehill, and Zida Borcich. I couldn't have made this book without you.

Marshall Rogers, my husband and truly a life partner, believed in me from the start. He never complained and insisted he was happy doing the cooking and cleaning while I worked at the keyboard. He is my proof that nearly perfect trust is possible.

To everyone who asked about the book, told me it was important, prayed for me, and shared their stories, thank you. I express my total gratitude to the clients who've honored me for over twenty years with their trust. Without their stories of tremendous courage, I would never have seen the importance of this book.

Introduction

Knowing when and how to trust others isn't easy. We enjoy the feelings of tenderness with people we respect and love. The shock of sudden betrayal or rejection causes a sense of belonging to suddenly disappear. The resulting pain and anxiety make us wonder if we'll ever want to trust again.

Trust is a factor in every interaction you have. You can be unaware of a conflict until your sense of trust is gone. A misunderstanding or a slight change in tone or mood can trigger a loss of trust. Fear and anger replace the feeling of belonging. You may pretend that everything is fine until the hard feelings fade or someone reaches out with warmth.

You are not limited to feeling like a helpless child or an angry parent when you feel betrayed. This book addresses the mystery that underlies upsetting interactions in many kinds of relationships. You'll be able to apply this book's principles and tools in both your romantic partnerships and work, and whether you are with parents, children, friends, or coworkers. The goal of this book is to encourage communication that conveys mutual respect and understanding.

This book is written to help anyone who's afraid to trust. You will find support and guidance whether you feel you trust too little or believe you trust the wrong people too easily.

Is It Ever Too Late to Learn to Trust?

Do you worry that painful experiences you had as a child can limit your ability to trust as a grown-up? Take heart. Children don't have the life experience to teach them that trust is more than a feeling that comes and goes under the control of other people. You have to be an adult before you can learn how to trust. Some people stay stuck in unhealthy patterns they learned as children, not knowing they can redesign the way they respond in difficult situations. You can learn to trust wisely.

This book offers information to build your self-confidence and help you to overcome your barriers to trust and intimacy. Each chapter addresses key issues about trust, intimacy, and betrayal. You'll begin by assessing your ability to trust yourself and others. As you move through the book, you'll gain specific information, and find exercises that help you do the following things:

- Increase your trust in yourself and your faith in a positive future.

- Identify your three core selves—the Child, the Protector, and the Adult—and their needs.

- Create intimacy by increasing mutual trust and understanding.

- Recognize when you overreact to felt betrayals and limit their power to undermine your self-worth.

- Acknowledge how you can betray others and how to undo the damage.

- End the cycle of self-betrayal that undermines the confidence to ask for what you want.

- Speak with compassionate honesty about the hurts you want to heal with another.

- Recognize when a relationship has too little trust and how to assess if it's time to go.

- Nurture the qualities that increase your own trustworthiness.

To trust is a choice you can make, and it is based on skills you can learn. Increasing your ability to trust is possible at any age, regardless of childhood history. The only way to increase your confidence is to practice certain skills and do whatever it takes to achieve the level of trust and intimacy you want. We all need courage to trust.

How to Get the Most from This Book

Track your progress by keeping a journal as you read along. Self-tests will give you a direct understanding of what is limiting your confidence in trusting yourself and others.

Go back to complete these questionnaires again as often as you wish to measure your progress. You can use the book's tools and exercises to work on real-life issues and enhance your ability to sort out misunderstandings and hurt feelings. You'll feel your self-reliance grow more quickly if you practice these skills in your daily life.

You may have a specific concern or an immediate need to focus on one topic. Although this book is designed to be read from start to finish, I encourage you to seek out any specific topics that will help you meet your challenges with the confidence that courage will bring.

CHAPTER 1

What Is Trust?

Why does it take courage to trust?

No one is born knowing how to trust. Life gives us many teachers, some caring and others cruel. Few people receive a solid base of trust as children. Even fewer are taught how to trust themselves. Regardless of the lessons we each received, we only learned *about* trust as children. We need to learn *how* to trust as adults.

We are not condemned by the limitations of our initial experiences. The ability to escape fears learned early on grows by challenging them. Trust is more than a mental state or feeling we can't control. Trust is a skill to be learned and a choice to be made. It is a gift to be shared with those who appreciate its importance.

Trust is also fragile and must be handled with great care. Careless words and impulsive actions can easily damage trust. Some decide early in life to seldom trust anyone, hiding their authentic self away from any possibility of rejection or betrayal. This is a safe but limited path.

This book encourages you to explore another path, one of learning how to trust wisely. Wisdom comes from taking the risk to reach out and trust others, while you know that you are likely to make some mistakes. This is where courage comes into play. Once you accept that you can learn from your mistakes, you'll find that trust in yourself will begin to grow.

Why It Takes Courage to Trust

It takes courage to confide in others. When you let down your guard in the hopes of a compassionate response, you take the risk that others may criticize you. With an unexpected shift of the emotional current, the door of tenderness is shut, and support transforms to attack. It's as if the oxygen was pulled from the room.

Ambivalence about trusting is based on the instinctive knowledge that no emotional state is guaranteed to last forever. If your caregivers were able to love and treasure you, an internal sense of safety was planted like a healthy seed. However, loss or betrayal at any time of life makes it difficult to develop or maintain an inner sense of confidence. Any traumatic event occurring in the first few years of life makes it harder to expand trust in others or yourself. Fear and uncertainty may persist as you grow. If the world seems filled with potential dangers, you will be tempted to limit how vulnerable you dare to be.

Confronting these limits takes deliberate and brave efforts. Those who had relatively painless childhoods will find that even the most trusted people can fail them. Friends and lovers get drunk and say stupid, unkind things. Lust runs over commitment. Employers make bad decisions and go bankrupt, costing you your job or future plans. Selfish desires often dominate promises made to others. People, animals, and dreams all eventually die.

Why should anyone bother to expand the ability to trust more deeply? Because when you trust wholeheartedly, it brings tremendous comfort and joy, even while you know it may not last forever.

Naming and Confronting Your Fears

This book outlines the hard work to confront the fears that limit trust. You can learn how and when to trust, even if you have been repeatedly betrayed. How? By admitting how much you fear being rejected if truly seen.

Almost everyone has found a way to hide their feelings, flaws, and dreams. Hiding your authentic self may be a means to avoid rejection, and seen as the only way someone could ever love you: "If others looked beneath my mask of confidence, they wouldn't want to know me."

Your instincts may tell you that your parents didn't love you for who you really are. How could someone love you if they

- abused you?

- frightened you?

- ignored or neglected you?

- criticized and shamed you?

- abandoned or rejected you, or died?

Self-doubt lingers even after we learn that our parents weren't perfect, and the problems they experienced weren't our fault. Parents who weren't loving and trustworthy could not teach a child to love and trust. This is why it is an adult task to learn to trust ourselves, and then to extend that gift to others.

In an ideal world, trust should be the standard, and betrayals would be unusual. Trust would rarely need to be discussed, because people would be honest. There would be a shared awareness of a greater good being served, and we would follow the rules we were given as children:

- Tell the truth, even when it hurts, for "honesty is the best policy."

- Keep your promises, since "a man is only as good as his word."

- "Think before you speak," because every word has power, and you can't ever take it back.

- "Look before you leap," for every action has consequences to others as well as yourself.

- Treat others as you would like to be treated—the Golden Rule of love applied to all.

We were exposed to these guidelines in an imperfect world and taught that good people obeyed them. We were punished when caught being unable to do so ourselves. Later we found out they were constantly broken by parents, teachers, and friends. Although the rules are based in common sense, they aren't in common practice.

We also quickly figured out that the rules were seldom enforceable, and many peers considered us foolish if we insisted on sticking to them. We were taken advantage of if we held to them ourselves: no one can win a game if everyone else is cheating. The immediate gratification of being accepted meant playing along.

A conflict between what we see and what we feel plays havoc on newly developing beliefs. This confusion is carried into adulthood and makes trust one of the most important riddles we have to solve.

If you are not sure what trust is, you're part of a very big club. We all hunger for the ability to trust others and to be seen as trustworthy. Let's begin with looking at what trust is.

What Is Trust?

Trust is a concept that rarely has a shared definition within the same family or intimate associations. Don't feel left out if you've never thought about what it means to you as an individual. Trust is not one-dimensional:

- Trust is a feeling.

- Trust is a choice.

- Trust is also a skill that can be learned.

Trust is the heartbeat of every significant relationship, with yourself as well as with others. We still want to trust despite disappointments in the past. Nothing flows without trust and love has no place to grow. You might be more aware of what trust feels like to you by its sudden disappearance. The scramble to regain trust shows what we feel we've lost and how important it is to feel understood.

The first step in learning how and when to trust is knowing when you are feeling trust.

Trust as a Feeling

There is a sense of safety and comfort when trust is present, and little inhibition. When asked to describe feeling trust in a relationship, people often recall being relaxed and calm: "I feel like I'm in the present moment, with no worry about our future together. There's no need to think about past problems." The return to trust after a disagreement feels like "we've erased the old resentments and can start fresh."

Self-Discovery Exercise: What Does Trust Feel Like?

Feelings are physical sensations that you have learned to identify. "Sadness," "happiness," and so forth are names we've given physical sensations. You'll learn to recognize the feeling you call "trust" by doing this exercise. It will be a touchstone for other exercises in this book, so do it now. It will take about ten minutes.

Note: Please read through the whole exercise before doing each step. This will reduce anxiety about what might be coming, and you'll get more from the process.

In your journal:

Make a short list of people whom you feel you can trust absolutely. Include people from your past, as well as today. If you find no one who fits this definition, please don't despair or quit. Just think of the person whom you trust the most or a beloved pet. Either will work.

Step 1. Choose one person and vividly recall a time when you were together. Feel what you think of as "trusting." Close your eyes and relax into the experience. Notice the way your body feels, including temperature, tension level, and the internal workings of your stomach, lungs, and heart.

Step 2. What makes you feel *safe* in the presence of this person? Ask, "What thoughts do I have about this being? How do I think he or she feels about me? How do I view our future together?" Follow these questions with "How does this person invite me to feel such trust: Is it a voice tone, words spoken, the way attention is given, a feeling of being important?" Add unique events that caused you to be certain you were safe.

Step 3. How do you feel about yourself when you are with this person? This is an important element of trust. Ask, "What is my view of my qualities and worthiness while with this person? What do I like about the way I am treating and speaking to him or her?" Mutual trust brings out the best in both of you, so notice how you feel about yourself as well as the other person.

Step 4. Write anything that feels important to capture. This is your grown-up impression of trust, and it will help you notice what elements of trust are present or absent in relationships you'll be exploring while reading this book.

Trust as a Choice

Choosing to trust can be so automatic that you don't even recognize when you made the decision. At other times, especially after heartbreak or betrayal, it feels impossible to trust anyone ever again.

You may be feeling a little anxious right now. You might have been taught that you had to trust, or pretend to trust, in order to avoid fights and hurt feelings. Placing blind trust in someone is dependency, not real trust. Consider the following scenario:

You are offered a ride to an event by a brand-new acquaintance who is a friend of a friend. You want to give the impression you trust the driver's skills, sobriety, responsibility, and the safety of the vehicle. But did you ask the driver about her driving history, how much she might have been drinking, or when the brakes were last checked? Probably not, because you don't want to seem rude and it would make you look controlling.

This is an example of pretending to trust, when you are dependent on someone without evidence of their being trustworthy. We do it in many different ways, seldom recognizing the opportunity to say no. How well do you handle this type of experience? When you go to a new doctor, do you worry more about appearing to be a good patient, rather than making certain their advice is appropriate for you? Many people are afraid of offending their doctor and neglect to get a second opinion, despite the dangers of proposed surgery or a lack of improvement with a severe problem. This isn't genuine trust—it is a form of dependency where the other person is the adult and you are the embarrassed child.

Conflict is often is difficult for adults to handle well, yet we are quick to criticize teenagers for getting into cars with other teens without screening them. "Why didn't you call me first?" Avoiding embarrassment can become life-threatening when you need to have the "safe sex" conversation with a new lover. One woman explained, "I didn't want him to think I didn't trust him when he told me about his negative HIV test and vasectomy." She didn't really trust him, but was afraid he'd reject her if she dared to care about her own life. "I trusted him enough to get naked and go to bed, but not enough to ask him to use a condom."

Some of the most dangerous interchanges in our culture are about driving, illness, and sex. We don't have permission or a common language to support that "trusting is always your choice." When you can fully embrace that you have the right to choose whether or not to trust someone, it is possible to make mutual agreements that suit each situation.

Pretending to trust hides the secret feeling that you are a frightened child sneaking into serious adult relationships. This can affect your role as a working person, as the adult child of parents who are critical and demanding, and as a friend.

You may have been rewarded for putting on a happy face, acting as if you love making sacrifices and aren't bothered by a lack of reciprocal respect. This could have caused you to seethe with inexpressible feelings or blow up, only to then sink back into the old situation. Telling yourself that "it doesn't matter, this too shall pass," didn't remove the pain. The events may have passed but the feelings of hurt and distrust lingered, ready to reignite the moment that the pattern is repeated.

You can change this without becoming an angry, demanding person if you learn to use your fears as a guide to what you really want out of your relationships. To do this, you will need to concentrate on developing the skills that no child can learn.

Trust as a Skill

There are two foundation skills that will increase your confidence about when, whom, and how much to trust. These skills give you the ability to define what you are feeling, and to find out what you want after experiencing a break in trust. The two trust skills are

1. *The Trust Check-In:* Privately acknowledge your thoughts, feelings, and needs without judgment or acting them out.

2. *Finding Out What You Want:* Ask yourself what you want from a situation, and what you are willing to risk to achieve it.

The Trust Check-In skill is introduced in chapter 2. Chapter 4 presents the second foundation skill: Finding Out What You Want. You'll have many opportunities in this book to practice these skills, to get more experience, and to gain awareness of how to apply them. Practicing these skills will challenge you to risk embarrassment and rejection. They will also contradict unhealthy habits and means of avoiding conflict.

It's tempting to seek the comfort of avoidance, even while you watch it suffocate some of your most important relationships. If you don't know what to do to make a relationship better, you may settle for what you have. This is a child's view of relationship; you didn't ask for the parents who raised you or for the various experiences that make you unique.

Although you might have been one of the lucky ones who saw trust consciously practiced by the grown-ups around you, no one can become adept with these skills as a child. No child can confront an adult who is self-absorbed and mean and tell him or her to be nice.

Types of Trust

The different types of trust we'll be exploring are *self-trust, faith in a positive future,* and *trusting others.* Each can serve you in many situations. One might be quite solid within your experience, and another might not have brought you the hoped-for sense of security. All can be strengthened to help you trust with increasing wisdom and confidence.

Self-Trust

To say "I trust myself" means you take care of your own needs and safety and are a loving force in your life. It requires a combination of the following beliefs:

- "I know what I am feeling and thinking, and can express it thoughtfully."

- "I follow an ethical code that sustains me, even though it's difficult at times."

- "I know when it is my job to take care of myself first, then to reach out to care for others."

- "Mistakes are often the best lessons. I can't avoid them, but I can pick myself up and try again."

- "I listen to all opinions and then decide for myself without needing to be right."

- "I know what I want and go for it in ways that don't limit others from doing the same."

It is scary to be truly honest with other people until you know you can count on yourself and know that you will survive if you have to be alone. Keeping your promises to yourself, as well as to others, is fundamental to building self-trust and achieving the independence necessary to feel like a real adult.

Self-trust supports your ability to explore new choices and tackle big challenges. It means opening to a bigger definition of who you really are and what you are capable of doing. The development of self-trust comes slowly. We are born without any internal dialogue about who we are and what we are worth. The people who surrounded us in early childhood gave us a dialogue that was repeated until we knew no other truth.

If you were frequently shamed, deliberately betrayed, or suffered significant loss in childhood, an inability to trust your feelings and perceptions may linger into adulthood. This can cause simple misunderstandings to trigger self-doubt and limit your ability to be open in your most important relationships. Changing beliefs about your worth is essential to developing high levels of self-trust.

Self-Discovery Questionnaire: How Much Do You Trust Yourself?

This questionnaire will help you identify your current balance of self-doubt and self-trust.

In your journal:

Keep a note of your score, since you'll want to return to this questionnaire as you go through this book and find out if you are increasing your self-trust. Jot down the questions that are particularly meaningful or distressing.

Give yourself a score of 0 to 5 for each question, where 0 means it doesn't apply at all, and 5 reflects a feeling or behavior that affects you often enough to be troublesome.

1. Do you berate yourself for having strong feelings (anger, fear, loneliness, or sadness) whether or not you show them to others?

2. Do you worry there is something secretly wrong with you, even if you don't know what it might be?

3. Do you often sacrifice your own needs for others?

4. Do you doubt that you are as capable or "good" as others think you are?

5. Do you hide your mistakes or minimize them?

6. Do you feel out of control about food, spending, drugs, or alcohol, but are too ashamed or afraid of failure to seek guidance or join a support group?

7. Do you think "I'm probably being selfish" when you consider asking others for a fair share of work or money, or extra help during times of stress?

8. Do you believe that others are more honest and open about what they think and feel?

9. Do you long to do something big (write a book, go to school, change your lifestyle) but seldom speak of it or explore what it would take to proceed?

10. Are you afraid you are failing this questionnaire?

Scoring: This questionnaire points to areas you might want to strengthen; it is not another means to pass or fail. Your first score gives you a baseline for this questionnaire. Complete it again a few times over the course of reading this book to see how you are changing.

31 to 50   Distrust of yourself is destroying your self-confidence.

20 to 30   Shows honest self-doubt; you could use more confidence.

0 to 19   You are very independent and self-confident.

Self-trust is not a steady state of self-confidence, immune to fears of failure and rejection. Self-doubt may tempt you to rely heavily on others' opinions. Learning to respect yourself will help you throw off old patterns of self-loathing. This will quiet the internalized voices of those who did not encourage you to believe in yourself.

The reward for becoming a more self-loving and responsible person is the opportunity to attract others who are learning to trust and like themselves. By increasing trust in yourself, you gather the courage needed to explore the second type of trust, faith.

Faith in a Positive Future

Faith in a positive future means a willingness to go forward, despite the risk of failure or loss. Faith in the face of uncertainty is based on a sense that there is something intrinsically good about life, people in general, and your own future. It is not dependent on a single situation, person, or belief. Faith appears when you offer your heart to the truth, opening to a kinder reality, even after terrible things have happened.

This form of trust is an expanded view of self-trust, and it is so individual that no example from others can perfectly match your experience. Sharon Salzberg has studied this topic from a personal and Buddhist perspective. In her book *Faith*, she offers this description: "No matter what we encounter in life, it is faith that enables us to try again, to trust again, to love again. Even in times of immense suffering, it is faith that enables us to relate to the present moment in such a way that we can go on, we can move forward, instead of becoming lost in resignation or despair. Faith links our present-day experience, whether wonderful or terrible, to the underlying pulse of life itself" (2002, XIV–XV).

Each of us has a measure of faith. We wouldn't be able to function without it. Driving on the highway requires faith that others are following the rules. Faith is such a basic orientation that most don't think of it as trust but more as a sense of knowing that everything is okay. We know we must die, yet are confident we'll awaken in the morning when we go to sleep at night. Faith is often taken for granted when we are not facing hardship.

When our faith in a greater good is challenged by a personal tragedy, we long for a reason and the faith that allows us to go forward. Victor Frankl, the psychiatrist who survived concentration camps and wrote *Man's Search for Meaning*, refers to this effort. Rabbi Kushner's *When Bad Things Happen to Good People* is a response to his reclamation of his faith after his son's death. The determination to return to a positive outlook demonstrates the level of faith that someone holds.

Practical Uses of Faith

Faith is not a belief to be taught or a mystical state of grace. It is something we *do*. From the earliest usage in many cultures, faith was considered an action. We act on faith when we deliberately envision good results in the face of uncertainty.

The practice of having faith enables you to name what you want and overcome to obstacles in achieving it. Faith keeps you from being paralyzed with fear of failure or rejection. A common misconception is that faith eliminates fear. It doesn't. Faith allows you to act despite fear. If you practice faith on the everyday challenges that make life interesting, you'll develop confidence in your ability to move forward into the uncertain future.

In your imagination, try tackling some of the things you'd like to do. Think about what scares you from making the attempt, then add a small statement of faith. Here are some examples to start you out:

- "I'd like to ask her out. I'll be embarrassed if she says no, but I'll survive."

- "I want to start my own business. I may not be instantly successful, but I'll learn as I go."

- "I've gained back my lost weight, but it's worth trying again. This time I'll get support."

This approach results in the kind of self-awareness that lets you seek the company of others who are self-assured and optimistic even when facing their own hard times. From them, you'll learn how to transform bad fortune and what seemed to be foolish mistakes into wisdom.

Trusting Others

Trusting others means relying on others' honesty and commitment to keep their promises to you. This is where you apply the first two types of trust. You will know when it's safe to trust someone else when you can read and trust your own feelings and have faith in a positive future. Trust is centered on the desire to trust others and to build satisfying relationships. Insecurities about how much you should trust are planted in your experiences since birth. The following questionnaire helps you reflect on how much you trust other people.

Self-Discovery Questionnaire: How Much Do You Really Trust Others?

Give yourself a score of 0 to 5 for each question, where 0 means it doesn't apply at all, and 5 reflects a feeling or behavior that affects you often enough to be upsetting.

In your journal:

Keep a note of your score, since you'll want to return to this questionnaire later to find if you are increasing your self-trust.

1. Do you believe people are upset with you, even when they say they aren't?

2. Do you feel insecure in telling others your goals, for fear they will judge you as incapable of achieving them or think you're conceited?

3. Do you avoid expressing preferences (food, driving safety, sexual pleasures) to your friends or partner, believing it will cause conflict or hurt their feelings?

4. Do you pretend to be "fine" about something that bothers you, even when honestly asked?

5. Are you reluctant to talk about how you handle money, even with professionals?

6. Do you announce your mistakes with great alarm, even exaggerate them?

7. Do you apologize for yourself more often than others seem to?

8. Do you fear others secretly judge or demean your appearance (body, speech, clothes)?

9. When people leave an abrupt message to call them or say, "I need to talk with you," are you afraid you did something to make them mad?

10. Do you believe you don't know how to have truly intimate relationships?

Scoring: Use your responses as pointers to areas to explore, rather than as another black mark on your character! Scoring gives you a baseline for this set of questions only. You'll want to retake this test midway through the book, then again at the end.

31 to 50   Your distrust of others is very high, limiting the depth of intimacy.

20 to 30   You want to trust others, but may experience more distrust than you admit.

0 to 19   You either trust people immensely, or you don't let them close enough to hurt you.

It's Never Too Late

So many of us believe that something is deeply wrong or broken inside of us. It is the only way to explain why people have hurt or rejected us. It follows that we also believe that our early experiences have destroyed our capacity to trust.

I know this isn't true. I once believed that my early hurts and betrayals were my fault. I thought they had to be kept secret for me to be loved and accepted by good people. My inner voices repeated the opinions of my worst teachers. There was another sense deep within me that doubted that the people who were mean and selfish knew the real me. I was attracted to kindness and tenderness, and moved toward those who were trustworthy and loving. And so I learned to trust and to love. Soon after, I learned how to become trustworthy and to receive love.

Revisiting early stories is scary, as is facing the feelings from those times. This book will give you the tools and support to change your story from one of betrayal to a life based on trust. It will help you to reconsider the beliefs that keep you from trusting yourself, having faith in a positive future, and choosing when it is wise to trust others.

Preparing for the Next Chapter

If you sometimes feel that there is an emotional tug-of-war inside you, you are not alone. We all have different selves, experienced as conflicted feelings or voices. In the next chapter, you will be introduced to the three core selves within you and within everyone.

You may have felt some echoes of early betrayals and pain while reading this chapter and taking the tests. The next chapter will help you understand and embrace the amazing way we have all learned to survive the hurts and come out on top, wanting to improve our ability to love and trust.

CHAPTER 2

Your Three Core Selves

Why do I sometimes act like a child?

Everyone has three core selves: the Child, the Protector, and the Adult. Their interrelationship works in harmony during ordinary moments. When you are feeling relaxed and in balance, it is because the Child feels safe, the Protector is tucked away calmly surveying the scene, and your Adult self is in charge. When trust feels threatened, you will acutely feel the separation among the three. Self-confidence is in short supply, and fear directs your actions.

The purpose of this chapter is to help you understand and align your inner selves after an upsetting event. This will give you a sense of being peaceful and capable. When you can count on connecting freely with your inner selves, you'll be grateful for the influence that each brings to your life.

This exploration will help you do these things:

- Learn how each of your core selves affects you mentally, physically, and emotionally.

- Discover what causes your core selves to split apart and learn how to tell who's in charge.

- Practice reconnecting with your Adult when trust has been broken.

You'll be introduced to the first·foundation skill, the Trust Check-In, at the end of this chapter. This is a powerful tool, one that puts your Adult back in control after upsetting interactions.

Who Are the Three Core Selves?

The Child can be playful, seeking belonging and tenderness with others. A sense of belonging meant survival during your early childhood. The desire for it continues throughout your life. When relationships feel threatened, the Child within you experiences self-doubt, shame, and fear.

The Protector steps in when the Child feels scared. It is quick to anger and pushes away anyone who may be causing harm. It also acts as an inner critic to avoid revealing too much. The Protector will even consider suicide when emotional pain seems intolerable. Your Protector is in charge when you feel strong anger, self-hate, or despair.

The Adult has the responsibility to make life work. No one can stay in their Adult all the time, but you can learn to return to your "right mind" more quickly after a split occurs. When you are feeling confidence and compassion, your Adult is in control. The Adult needs the Child and Protector to keep life in perspective.

The Needs and Goals of Each Self

The balance of the three core selves defines much of your personality. In chapter 7, you'll have the opportunity to delve more deeply into your own unique patterns of reaction and thought. For now, here is a summary that will help you understand the way most people experience their three core selves.

How the Child Self Is Shaped

Everyone is born with the instinct to reach out in the presence of tenderness and pull away from discomfort and pain. Emotions are unformed in infancy, and sensations are limited to variations of fear and contentment. The infant or toddler senses the danger of being alone when the mother leaves the room, and erupts into crying for help. When a parent returns and holds the child, all is right with the world.

As language and motor skills grow, children take in everything they see and hear, and model their behavior on those around them. If others tell you you're good, you're good. If they tell you you're bad, you're bad. Unfortunately, there can be too many versions of "you're bad" from parents, teachers, and siblings. Consider this list:

- "Grow up! Stop being such a child."

- "Don't be such a baby—it doesn't hurt that much."

- "Stop crying or I'll give you something to cry about."

Children are not intellectually capable of discriminating between negative and positive. This confusion plants the seed of "there must be something wrong with me." This belief gets locked in early and influences everything that comes later.

Even adults who seem to glow with self-confidence have moments where they doubt their competence and worth. Most children idealize adults as models of self-assurance. As children, we long to grow up, start our periods or grow a beard, and drive a car. These symbols connect to the fallacy that "when I grow up, I'll be sure of myself and not care what anyone thinks."

Growing up and becoming self-reliant requires tolerating ever-increasing time alone. Having to live without constant support and attention is a big part of what makes becoming an adult so difficult. We learn this consciously as we mature, but that doesn't mean we can tell our nervous systems to be calm when faced with the possible loss of someone we care about.

How the Child Self Shows in Adults

Our sense of belonging can be quite fragile. Something as minor as being told your pants are unzipped or being teased about a mistake can render your Adult self incapable of holding on to self-confidence. This is evidence of your helpless Child appearing.

Reassurance by others won't instantly turn off this defensive reaction. The Child feels panic about an event that the Adult could otherwise recognize as a temporary embarrassment. The perception of the Adult is swamped by the Child's need to escape from the pain of rejection. This experience is compounded when someone is angry or neglecting us and can bring up old fears of being unlovable.

When you are unable to stand up against people who are unfair, your frightened Child is dominating you. It can be especially disconcerting when you feel competent in other areas but cannot break free of the feelings of powerlessness in important relationships. The Protector springs to the rescue when the Child is overwhelmed with fear and helplessness.

How Your Protector Serves You

We have an innate part that responds to any threat to survival. This developing self pays close attention to the people who are sources of tenderness and pain. Existence depends on increasing our ability to keep out of harm's way. To do this, children need to learn to fit in and follow instructions. The Protector comes alive during the "terrible twos," and we start to practice self-reliance around three years old. Our fragile confidence must be defended against the pointed criticism: "What is *wrong* with you?"

There is a blessed limit to how much criticism children can take. Children learn to survive the blows and nonstop lectures on their flaws, and the Protector secretly begins to gain influence. Many figure out that anger and hate counteract fear and make them feel powerful.

Knowing when you are angry and hurt is framed in "right and wrong" and "fair and unfair." The Protector acts as judge against anyone who scares or hurts the Child. It may want to destroy—at least in imagination—anyone who tries to harm or humiliate the Child.

The Protector holds the will to survive and makes it possible to separate from others. The Protector holds the inner strength that allows you to survive incredible pain, abuse, and ridicule. Inner dialogue often runs to the extreme:

- "I'll show them!"

- "I'll be perfect. I'll never make another mistake."

- "I won't let them see me cry, even when they hit me."

- "I'll run away or kill myself, and then they'll be sorry."

As you grow, the Protector develops new ways to keep you safe, denying pain and minimizing your feelings. Other techniques to numb bad feelings are added as you become more independent. Overeating, drugs, and forbidden relationships give a sense of immediate relief, regardless of the eventual negative consequences.

The Jobs of the Protector

Your Protector reacts to possible rejection or hurts. It also performs these functions:

The Protector remembers the bad stuff. The Protector locks away upsetting memories, often for years, until something triggers their release. These are called *flashbacks*:

- A rape victim sees someone who resembles her attacker, and faints or becomes ill.

- Survivors of sexual abuse become panicked or numb when touched without permission.

- Adults yelled at as children accuse their partners of yelling when they speak strongly.

- The request to "have a talk" causes acute anxiety to those who were frequently shamed.

Until memories are given a safe place to be explored, the Protector continues to react to triggering events. If you sense something may have happened to you but are afraid to find out, be gentle with yourself and know it is fine to go at your own pace. Someday you'll know it is time, and you'll find the person who can give you the guidance you need.

The Protector seeks instant comfort. We often first acknowledge the power of our Protector when feeling powerless to make positive changes. Here are some examples:

- feeling stuck in an unhealthy relationship

- when you can't stop overeating, smoking cigarettes, or abusing drugs and alcohol

- having angry outbursts that hurt those you love

- experiencing anxiety or phobias that limit the courage to reach out and express yourself

You may wonder why you fall back into old destructive habits when you experience emotional pain. This automatic response is triggered by the powerful need for the Child to be comforted. If your Adult self cannot reassure and address the fears of the Child, the Protector will jump in to stop the pain. Unfortunately, the Protector cares nothing about long-term consequences and will use the most immediate means to soothe fears of rejection and prevent you from making a positive change. These instant comforts are often unhealthy. In chapter 6, you will have a chance to explore how you may fall into this pattern and learn new ways to work with your Protector.

How the Protector Keeps You Safe

There are four primary responses to stress: fight, flight, freeze, and faint. Your Protector learned to react to pain by observing the ways you were treated as a child:

- If you identified with a parent who raged, you may be hot tempered and often scare others with your anger.

- If you escaped hurts by running away, you may now avoid conflicts by refusing to talk.

- If you were told to "sit down and shut up" and were then lectured at, you may freeze if anyone gets upset with you.

- If you were beaten or molested, you may leave your body under stress, going into a kind of trance.

It is possible for the same situation to evoke fight, flight, freeze, or faint in different people. Recognizing the response you learned as a child helps you to calm the Child and understand the Protector. You probably have experienced each of these responses at various times, but everyone has a predominant style and the following questionnaire will help you find yours.

Self-Discovery Questionnaire:
How Do You Protect Yourself?

Recall a recent situation when you thought someone was angry or rejecting. Examples: when you felt unfair blame, when you perceived disrespect, when you had a feeling you had been betrayed. Use a scale of 0 ("Not me!") to 5 ("Are you reading my journal?") to reflect how well the following responses describe your reaction to that situation.

Fight

_____ *I get angry so fast, I can't control it. I might break something or hit someone.*

_____ *My heart instantly hardens. I feel cold, unloving.*

_____ *My whole body gets hot. I want to jump up and scream.*

Flight

_____ *I'm out of here! I might even leap from a moving car if it's bad enough.*

_____ *I want to just walk away. I think I never want to see the other person again.*

_____ *I can't stop talking. My mind is going a million miles an hour.*

Freeze

_____ *My mind is a blank. I can't think of a thing to say.*

_____ *I feel punched in the stomach, unable to move or talk.*

_____ *My heart is beating fast. My mouth is dry. I feel like a robot.*

Faint

_____ *I can't remember what the other person said.*

_____ *My body feels like Jell-O. My knees buckle and I can't stand up.*

_____ *I just wait until the bad part stops, then act like nothing has happened.*

Scoring: Add up your scores in each of the four categories. Rank your Protector's responses to stress from most common to least common response for you.

In your journal:

There are no good or bad patterns. Just note what yours are in your journal. Reflect on times in the past when you may have reacted differently from how you do now. There may be situations where you have responded in another way. What was different about the situation, your emotional state? Were the stakes higher? Were they lower?

Example: I often saw anger lead to violence when I was a child. As a result, I made a choice to never get angry. Now I can admit I am angry, but don't act it out. I shut down and freeze up. It's better now; I can unfreeze more quickly and admit out loud, to myself first, when I am hurt and angry. My current order of reaction: 1. Freeze; 2. Flight; 3. Faint; 4. Fight.

Complete this self-questionnaire again when you have finished reading this book. You may find that your ranking is similar, but the intensity of your responses is more moderate. It is possible you'll find your reactions have shifted to a different mode.

The Protector responds the instant that the Child feels bad about him- or herself. It can't assess if the cause makes sense or if the comforts it chooses are wise. That is the job of the Adult.

Your Adult Can Grow Wiser Every Day

It's tempting when looking back on childhood to wish away foolish actions. Many of us still cringe when recalling a humiliating incident of youth. "If only I knew then what I know now!" This thought is a leftover from early messages of "act your age." We only learn by trying new ideas and making mistakes. Confidence comes after mistakes are repeated with many variations over a long life.

Your Adult self starts to develop in the early teen years. Independence from the original tiny circle of childhood offers a larger view of yourself and what you can dare to try. New insights and ideas allow you to challenge the self-doubt you were taught by any mean-spirited and small-minded people in your childhood. Parents can't stay your primary source of safety and belonging. As a teenager, you are just now capable of deciding whether or not someone feels trustworthy.

Adult qualities begin to show up in the late teens and you start practicing them in your early twenties. You get to make some bad choices and learn from them. Wanting to be wise and successful, you explore theories and seek teachers who point in those directions. With adult thinking comes self-confidence.

Qualities that indicate a high self-confidence and mature thinking are

- empathy and compassion, eventually including those who have hurt you

- forgiveness for yourself and others; releasing past pain and shame

- taking responsibility for what happens in your life by recognizing cause and effect

- accepting that there are many sides to every story; wanting to hear others' perceptions

- the ability to release bad habits and walk away from people who can harm you

- recognizing that you can survive and learn from difficult times

No one can ever perfect these qualities. Accepting that you and others aren't perfect comes as we grow older and wiser. If your early life was filled with self-destruction, it is important to know that it is never too late to start working on self-confidence and mature thinking.

Some people don't seem interested in being competent adults. They reject responsibility and cling to childish self-interest. Their Protector is constantly on duty. These adult children will defend self-destructive habits and frequently rage at those they believe are victimizing them. There is little chance they'll develop trust or faith, or have others trust them.

Strengthening the Adult

The Adult holds the courage to act in spite of feeling anxious or uncertain. This is the face you present to the world. The Adult plans and sets goals, reads self-help books, goes to work, talks thoughtfully with friends, and pays the bills. This is the socialized self who looks for meaning in life and strives to not take things too personally.

Your Adult is the inventor and guardian of your life's choices. Faith-based philosophies view this self as the part of you that can link to your "higher self," or a higher power. The Adult is able to develop real faith. After being shattered by failure or betrayal, your adult works hard to pick up the pieces and eventually try again. Sharon Salzberg highlights the Adult capacity to believe in your "immense potential, and to be free of the habits of anguish and fear" (2002, 10).

One measure of a strong Adult is emotional resilience. This supports you in the face of uncertainty. You can trust yourself to do the right thing and learn from mistakes. To get an idea of how emotionally resilient you are, try the following questionnaire, adapted from an article by Danielle Palmer (2003):

Self-Discovery Questionnaire: How Well Do You Handle Uncertainty and Rejection?

This questionnaire will help you identify how quickly your Adult self responds with resilience to perceived rejection or uncertainly.

In your journal:

It is perfectly natural for everyone to have an initial wave or reactivity from the Child or Protector selves with a major shock or perceived rejection. Note the scores you give yourself, from 0 to 5: zero describes a low ability to tolerate the described experience, 5 shows a high degree of Adult influence to offer a resilient and larger perspective.

1. When under pressure and deadlines, do you deliberately seek techniques to help keep you calm and thinking clearly?

2. Do you identify obstacles or unpredictable changes as challenges, seeking creative outcomes?

3. In a tight or scary situations, do you believe that help is likely to come?

4. In stressful situations, do you feel excited and confident, knowing that you'll rise to the challenge?

5. When you make an honest mistake, do you deliberately work to release the self-anger, or focus instead on how to learn from your misjudgment?

6. In tight situations, are you able to focus on the challenge, avoiding distraction or negative thoughts?

7. When you fell the need to stand up for yourself and what you believe, are you confident you'll speak your truth?

8. Are you willing to take on new or challenging opportunities, even though stressful?

9. When life gives you hardship and pressure, do you work to release tension and hope for positive resolution, or do you obsess on negative or threatening possibilities?

10. When you don't know what to do, are you able to reach out to others, even enjoying asking for guidance and support?

Scoring: Add up your numbers and compare to the following assessment for the Adult's resiliency. What you are measuring here is the ability of your adult self to step in and influence your behavior and thoughts after the initial shock or surprise has passed, or when the pressure continues.

39 to 50   You seek a bigger picture, using internal and external resources to find positive outcomes.

26 to 38   Although you handle difficult situations, stress and self-doubts may linger longer than is productive.

10 to 25   You may get stuck in unsafe or unhealthy situations, seeing only the problem, feeling inadequate to seek resolution.

Keep note of this score in your journal so you can take the questionnaire again as you gain resiliency. No one gets a perfect score—it is more meaningful to acknowledge where your confidence and resilience are currently strong or need more support. Your Adult self does best when it knows what problems to address. If your score seems especially low, perhaps you were hard on yourself. Try again on a day when you are feeling more confident. Ask a trusted friend to answer the questionnaire and discuss his or her responses together. Should you continue to feel troubled by your answers, talk it over with a counselor or minister.

When the Selves Split Apart

It happens in an instant. You're feeling warm and confident. Then there is a sudden shift in a conversation. You feel a shiver of fear, and tenderness is replaced with tension. If the distance is bridged with a quick apology or explanation, you put your sensibilities back in proper order. You can take a full breath again, and you begin to relax your guard.

The three selves are put on alert when there is no mollifying response to calm your fear. You might try to sort it out by asking the other person, "What just happened? Are we okay?" The Adult wants a rational response to bridge the gap. The Child is quaking and your voice may reveal it.

Should you not feel safe enough to ask, or there is no response, you are left with reviewing what happened alone. You are likely to find yourself teetering between being angry and wondering what you did wrong. Thoughts and feelings come fast and contradict each other. There is a danger of overreacting. This is because your three selves are out of balance, and the Adult is no longer in charge.

"Why Was I So Childish and Mean?"

Twenty-two-year old Judy and her older sister, Penny, were opening presents on Christmas morning, along with some family friends. The girls' parents had been killed in an auto accident two years before, and they were trying to re-create a new sense of family. Christmas morning had always been a favorite tradition, everyone trying to surprise and outdo each other with different gifts, and Judy was excited to share a happy time with her sister again. She'd worked hard to get Penny the perfect present.

Judy described what happened that morning with now fading embarrassment: "Penny opened her gift and was delighted. I just knew that Penny had bought me the new computer I needed for my graphics class. A big box had been camouflaged by smaller packages under the tree for a couple of days. It was just the right size. But when I went to unwrap the box, it weighed next to nothing. It couldn't be a computer, and I dropped it in shock. I screamed right in Penny's face, 'I hate you! How could you do this to me?' I burst into tears, and ran into the bathroom and locked the door. I sobbed and raged, and even threw things. I stayed there for half an hour, refusing to listen to Penny or our friends.

"When I finally emerged, Penny was crying, and our friends were distant. Penny had ordered me a special computer and it hadn't come in time, so she had put the brochure in a computer box along with high-end graphics software. I spoiled Christmas. I couldn't eat or pull out of the depression. Our friends left early, not saying much. Penny and I hugged. She said she understood and forgave me, but I got sick every time I thought about it. I know now my reaction was mainly about Mom and Dad not being there, and I guess my little kid inside was scared to feel them gone. But it terrified me that I got so mean and hateful. I'd never done anything like that before!

"At first, I hated myself and wanted to die. Then, with Penny's loving encouragement, I talked it through. I saw that my Child had built up hopes for a perfect Christmas to avoid the sadness of missing Mom and Dad. My Adult was trying to hold it together, but my little kid felt so betrayed, I lost control. My Protector got me away from the grief by focusing on anger. I easily forgave Penny, as well as our friends for not being able to stay. It took me longer to forgive myself. I called our friends that same night and explained why I reacted the way I did. They were great. They said that hearing the whole story helped them understand and trust me again."

Splits like this occur within us almost every day. Most fade quickly, but when the Adult cannot reassure the Child quickly enough, the Protector steps in to make the pain go away. We feel a small slight as a stab in the heart. We can obsess that we've blown an entire relationship with a thoughtless comment. Fear and rage are the hallmarks of the Child and Protector, and they counterbalance the Adult's ability to hold onto trust.

We are remarkably adept at hiding these splits from one another, appearing to shrug off the hurt and fear. However, inside we are fuming or berating ourselves. It takes skill and patience to invite the Adult back into control.

Putting the Adult Back in Charge

New skills are needed to increase your emotional resiliency and return responsibility to your Adult. Once you learn to calm your Child rather than to overreact in situations, your Protector will adapt and embrace positive defenses.

The Trust Check-In skill reassures and calms both your Protector and Child. This template will guide you in exploring the feelings that currently cause confusion. You can then gently reassert the Adult back into leadership. You'll start to see healthy options to problems and find the courage to speak honestly about what you want to happen.

When Something's Not Right

You know when something's not right in a relationship. The clues are that your mind won't stop badgering you and your emotions are swinging wildly. Self-doubt often makes it difficult to talk with someone else, so you are left to brood or try to talk yourself out of being upset. The doubt leads to anxiety or anger, sometimes expressed in an unfortunate manner.

This means that you've lost trust with yourself or another. The Trust Check-In helps you sort out the problem and decide if there is anything you want to do or say.

First Foundation Skill: The Trust Check-In

Read the following all the way through before beginning this exercise. There's an example at the end to give you more direction. Once you've gone through this process a few times, you can complete it in less than twenty minutes—even less for minor incidents. Take your time at first, and give yourself at least a half hour. Have your journal nearby.

Step 1. Feel and name upsetting emotions. Recall a recent incident where you felt split and unable to keep your emotional balance. It might have started with an interaction with someone, or you may have experienced sudden anxiety or a flashback. Close your eyes and recall the whole story. See it as if you were there right now.

Feel every physical sensation that arises. Don't block the hard ones. Let your body remind you of the discomfort you felt at the time. Stomach tight? Heart beating fast? Are you holding your breath? Inviting the sensations to wash over you releases much of their power and control.

Name *out loud* the emotions that go with the sensations. Essential emotions are anger, sadness, fear, guilt, and shame. Ask for each in turn. Start with "I am angry at [myself, them] because . . ." "I am sad that . . ." Then follow with fear, guilt, and shame. Feel and say whatever comes up. If you are afraid to feel anger, slow down and ask gently, "If I did feel anger, it would be at . . . because . . ."

In your journal:

Step 2. Write down all your feelings. Please take this important step. Feelings will retain power until you write them down. You'll diminish their sway by writing out your responses.

Honor the Child's feelings: Complete either of these sentences as many times as you need. "My Child self is . . . [or] I am feeling . . ." Imagine if you had an actual child sitting with you. Wouldn't you encourage the child to talk about what is bothering him or her? Child selves get scared beyond reason and tend to recall minor incidents with exaggerated shame. They want the pain to stop and everyone to like them again. Write down the feelings in about four sentences. Be gentle. Pause for two deep breaths, then turn your attention to the Protector.

Ask what the Protector has to say, listening without censorship: Here comes the anger, wanting to minimize your part or make it all the other's fault. Fight, flight, freeze, or faint? What does the Protector want to do to stop your Child's pain? Is it criticizing you for getting into a mess again? Let it flow. Write hard and fast, reliving those feelings. You need to know what is boiling up inside in order to return to your Adult. Pause, breathe. Let the calm settle over you, and then open to your Adult.

Invite the Adult's view: Look for the faith, a larger perspective: "This, too, shall pass. I will take responsibility for my part and consider what happened to the other(s). If the relationship is damaged, I can handle it. I will do what I can and have faith we both will be okay."

Step 3. Write a short letter to the Child and the Protector from the viewpoint of your Adult. You will ease the Adult back in charge by speaking from this position. The Child wants everything to be okay again, and the Protector just wants you to be safe. Your Adult knows healing may take some time, and it might be best to create space, even if this is upsetting to the Child. Ideas and suggestions will surface only after the fear, anger, and despair have been fully explored. Breathe.

Example:

Kelly was in a training session for elementary school teachers. It included a simple art project as an exercise. She became violently anxious when she started to draw, and told the instructor that she was feeling ill so she could leave the session. "I know the problem was emotional because I was fine the instant I got home. Something to do with the drawing forced me to leave. I was enjoying myself up until that moment."

Kelly said that she liked to draw as a child, but admitted, "I never pursued doing more art. I just didn't have the discipline." Still, the intensity of her anxiety was compelling enough to seek out the reason for it. She used the Trust Check-In, listening for the voices of her Child and Protector, asking, "What made me so scared about drawing?"

Kelly remembered that she had more than a passing interest in art. Her parents had given her real art supplies for her eighth birthday, and then for her ninth had enrolled her in a drawing class for advanced students. At age ten she made her very best drawing, using a book of anatomy and models. "It was of two dancers wearing ballet slippers and little else. When my mother saw the drawing, she nearly choked, and tore it out of my sketch book." Her mother took it to their priest, who deemed it to be bordering on sinful and not a good path for a young girl. The result was that Kelly was pulled from the class. Despite her pleas, Kelly was banned from the class, and her art supplies were burned.

Her mother believed she had to stop Kelly from drawing to save her very soul. Controlling parenting became the model for Kelly's protector. "It was the Protector who didn't let me draw again, even when I was an adult." The Protector was locked in with her ten-year-old self, and prevented the risk of Kelly being so shamed ever again.

Kelly laughed as she recalled a recent visit with her mother that had puzzled her at the time. Her mother was telling a visitor how artistically talented her daughter had been as a child, and asked, "Why didn't you ever continue with your art? You were so talented and we spent extra money on you for art class." Kelly wondered, "I felt angry, then ashamed, but hid it. I couldn't figure out why I was 'overreacting,' so I said, 'I was just lazy, I guess.' "

Kelly's Trust Check-In:

My Child is feeling ashamed about the way I came apart at the training. She is also afraid that I'll get in trouble if I start to draw again. She's really stuck at being ten years old. My Protector is furious at my mother, but it has also kept me quiet all these years. I'm upset that my mother forgot about it, or is playing innocent for her absurd overreaction. Drawing was so important to me. How could she have done that?! I am really angry about that!

Kelly's letters:

Dear little Kelly: You didn't do anything wrong. Of course, you had to stop drawing, because Mommy said so. Now we can try it again. You are a wonderful artist and deserve to have fun again. I'm sorry I didn't know how to keep this from being awful for you for all these years, and for putting you into this new class that scared you so much. I love you.

Dear Protector: Wow, were you clever about how you got me out of that class! Thank you for keeping me safe all these years. I'd like to try to draw again, and will do it alone first before I take a class. I promise I won't let the little girl get in trouble. It's okay now. Thank you.

Preparing for the Next Chapter

The idea of getting really close to someone delights your Child but scares your Protector. Your Adult needs to keep both reassured that being open won't become a threat to your survival. To get ready for more intimacy, practice the Trust Check-In on issues with older relationships.

In the next chapter, you'll have a chance to view your current relationships in terms of trust and belonging. Your Adult will have the opportunity to think about the people you want to be closer to, and those you might want to distance.

CHAPTER 3

Trust Is the Pathway
to Intimacy

Why is it so hard to create intimacy?

It's healthy to long for a sanctuary where you can safely reveal your Child's fears and Adult dreams. Intimacy can be this safe place, but it isn't created instantly. Mutual honesty and understanding are the foundations of real intimacy. Even with these, intimacy can disappear for long periods. It's hard work and takes solid self-trust to build intimacy between two people.

You must be vulnerable to have closeness with someone. This is where you share your innermost self. Your Adult chooses whom to entrust with the Child's tender secrets and fears.

What Is Healthy Intimacy?

Intimacy deserves a very personal definition. For some, it is the closeness they feel when someone listens to their dreams. Others find intimacy by sharing their turmoil, feeling support as evidence of deep connection. Sometimes we don't consciously choose the moment when we reveal ourselves. We have few defenses when our hearts are broken and will show hidden weakness in our grief. Intimacy is created when we are tenderly met at such times.

The pathway into lasting intimacy begins with knowing and accepting yourself. Until you are ready to love yourself in your current state of imperfection, you can't expect others to do so. Intimacy flourishes when mutual respect is grounded in self-respect. Each step toward intimacy takes the courage to let go of judging yourself and others.

The confidence to reveal your innermost thoughts and feelings increases with the degree of belonging and intimacy. Opening yourself in this way also means uncovering conflicts that can't be glossed over. The desire for mutual acceptance builds healthy intimacy.

Building Blocks of Healthy Intimacy

Healthy intimacy is achieved when you consciously develop these qualities and commitments:

- telling the truth with the Adult's compassion

- asking for what you want, even when it scares the Child

- a willingness to listen with an open mind and accepting that you might be wrong

- an agreement to speak up when hurt and a promise of tenderness in response

- acknowledging the overreactions of your Protector and making meaningful amends

- having the faith that you both will be okay even if one wants to separate

These are guidelines for exploring your own definition of intimacy. Even in the most solid of relationships, it takes courage to reach out and try again when you have felt betrayed. Intimate sharing feels like the last thing you should try for. This is why you need to strengthen your emotional resilience and self-reliance. Then you can trust yourself to stay openhearted when someone you care about disagrees or is angry with you.

Intimacy is strengthened every time differences are discussed and you take the risk to revisit difficult topics. The joy of steadfast intimacy comes after you have exposed deep truths and accept and understand each other.

Barriers to Intimacy

Anything that stops you from sharing freely about yourself creates a barrier to intimacy. Few of us were taught how powerful it can be simply to say what we feel and ask for what we want.

Children are too often expected to magically know the right thing to do or what is expected of them. Accusations are delivered in tirades of anger and sometimes accompanied with physical punishment. Such scenes are frequently followed with a message that this is done out of love for the child.

As children, we learn to bend to others' needs and are not encouraged to ask for what we really want. Rather than speaking freely, we learn to hold back our truths, listening for clues about what others want to hear. Our real stories, with secrets both wonderful and awful, are hidden from others' judgments by years of denial. Healthy intimacy is impossible in such a state.

Intimacy is sabotaged by self-doubt, leading us in these wrong directions:

- *enmeshment*, which causes us to sacrifice our needs for people who are incapable of returning our respect

- *instant intimacy*, which invites betrayal and reinforces the idea that something is wrong with us

- *idealizing others*, which disguises low self-esteem as we rely on others to affirm our worth

Enmeshment Causes You to Sacrifice Yourself

Enmeshment is the complex of feelings and beliefs that causes you to stay in a situation to please someone else. Your needs become secondary to the survival of the relationship. One way into this trap is the conviction that you have to stay because the other person loves you and claims that life without you would be unthinkable. Another way is for the other person to persuade you that you couldn't make it without him or her. A deal between you is made early in the relationship. The result is that you end up denying your own dreams and goals.

If this is your story, your Child self was taught to consider others first, even when you are miserable. You may feel ready to leave, but you cannot bear breaking the heart of another. It becomes impossible for you to leave a dead-end job because you are so worried that coworkers will be mad at you. You feel compelled to sacrifice your future to take care of aging parents who could fend for themselves. This is not the route to take to create an intimate relationship.

You may believe you love someone, but if you engage in the following behaviors, it means you have lost trust in the other person. Do you recognize any of these internal conflicts in an important relationship?

- You complain to other people who aren't involved, but you won't talk to the person whose behaviors upset you.

- You assume that asking for what you want will end in a fight, or it will embarrass you both.

- You criticize each other, but you minimize or deny the problems when confronted.

- You don't know how to ask for closeness. It's easier to say, "I'm sorry I said anything, rather than pursuing the issue."

- The thought of losing a relationship stops you from trying to improve it. "I can't get another divorce! It's not always this bad. After all, he puts up with my moods."

These examples show a lack of self-respect for your feelings and needs. Intimacy is impossible when you let someone else control the level of honesty in your relationship. The other person knows you're afraid to insist on resolving conflicts because you've never carried out your threats to leave, get counseling, or pursue your dreams.

Eventually, you will realize that the other person has no investment in making changes. Perhaps you'll see that he or she can't. When you feel this hopeless, you know deep down that it would be in your best interest to separate. You are enmeshed if you think you need the other person's permission to leave.

Needy partners often become abusive of those they depend on. It is their Protector's efforts to hide fears of inadequacy. Abusive or demanding people must be in relationships with partners who believe they can't leave them. Enmeshment meets their Child's needs to be accepted, no matter what they do (Brown 2001). This important topic of loving those who hurt you is explored further in chapter 9.

"I Didn't Believe I Could Take Care of Myself"

Gisela escaped her upper-class European background by going to India to do volunteer work and to study spiritual practices. She had never been taught to be self-supporting, only to be artistic and beautiful. Her fantasy was to find a clever and loving husband to care for the practical things.

She met Robert, an American who lived by his wits and who was very loving and intelligent. They married and settled in the United States, where they built a home and had two children. Gisela gladly let Robert manage her inherited money. He went to school but kept shifting careers, looking for one that stayed exciting. He loved the international scene and sought ventures that could be lucrative and meaningful. None made much money, but they gave him contacts with powerful people and the feeling of being important.

Every few years, Gisela tried to talk with Robert about changing to a life of simplicity and less expense. Their different values and her need for financial security were obvious, but he kept reassuring her that things were fine and that he was looking out for their future. He promised that the next deal would settle all their debts. "You just need to trust me. I love you and would never do anything to hurt you." He would delight her with exciting stories of his travels and meetings.

For years, Robert's confidence overpowered Gisela's doubts. When a mortgage payment was missed, she decided to take a careful look at their financial papers, and it seemed to her that Robert wasn't being realistic. She couldn't bring up her lack of trust in him, however, because she feared he would leave and she'd be forced to raise their two children alone. She talked about their money problems with friends, who encouraged her to get financial advice and develop her skill in managing money. She began to study business and got a job. Robert reacted with disdain at what Gisela was learning.

After fifteen years of marriage, their debts were as big as their assets. Gisela insisted to Robert that they get financial counseling. Either he would work with her to turn their problems around, or she would divorce him. He refused.

Gisela recalls this moment, "I took a stand, and for the first time I felt strong enough to separate." Gisela's lack of self-reliance and Robert's denial of her ideas and needs had taken a toll on their intimacy.

Gisela saw a lawyer and made the necessary legal changes to protect her remaining assets. "I'm now free to do things as they make sense to me. I love Robert, but I couldn't see him for who he was. I blindly trusted his competence and doubted my own. We were both children, living in dreams. Robert is still hoping for the next big deal, refusing to buy into my plans. I want to be a responsible adult and take care of myself in a way that is true to my values: simply, without debt, and joyfully, without fear. I see now that allowing myself to be overshadowed by a male authority against my own conviction was my biggest mistake."

Instant Intimacy Invites Betrayal

People can suddenly jump into your life with such intensity that it overpowers all safe boundaries and your good sense. This heartfelt connection can last for a plane trip, one magical night, or an exhilarating month. The person plunges deep into your life and then leaps out, leaving you filled with a confusion of emotions and sometimes regrets. Common experiences of instant intimacy include

- love at first sight, then realizing it was only infatuation

- impulsive sex that later brings shame and possible dire consequences

- using drugs and/or alcohol together, especially compulsively

- deep sharing at spiritual gatherings, personal growth groups, or workshops

In these circumstances, it is easy to reveal and promise too much. You may find yourself wishing you could undo the whole thing. You may be afraid of losing control over your life. Deep down, you know the relationship can't work and that you'll soon be free. The Child in you craves the illusion of total acceptance. The Adult knows it is dangerous and temporary: relationships like these seldom last.

Those who search for a soul mate in bars or in online chat rooms are trying to hide their imperfect selves. The "hurry up and let's get to the real stuff" avoids the torture of revealing your flaws. There is the desperate hope that sex and extraordinary efforts to please others will make them love you, despite your perceived imperfections. "Maybe you'll want me if I prove how perfectly I can love you."

If you are mentally naming your children on the second date, you can little afford to notice or want to comment on areas that scream of incompatibility. Intimacy demands the slow unfolding of your secrets and doesn't thrive in casual relationships. You may feel hints of intimacy when someone tells you a painful story and lets you comfort his or her scared Child. However, the fear of commitment, of being swallowed up and controlled, brings an awkward end to momentary closeness.

Idealizing Others Hides Low Self-Worth

We're all attracted to people who are physically attractive, talented, or powerful. They have such self-assurance. Our tendency is to invent entire stories about them, where we imbue them with fabulous characteristics. We believe that if someone extraordinary accepts us, it proves we're okay. The feeling of bliss at this person's acceptance is mistaken for intimacy: "I've never felt so good, so loved, so beautiful. This is the real thing."

People who "come on strong"—whether lovers, new bosses, or clergy—present their ideas with enchanting self-confidence. Some even deliberately play to your insecure Child, who is ready to leap into their arms, cubicles, and pews, unable to see obvious risks. Intelligent women fall for "bad boys," and insecure men are attracted to women who flirt and break hearts with abandon. Warnings are unheeded by the Child, who longs to eradicate long-held feelings of inadequacy.

Things seldom go the way you'd hope: the CEO runs away with the funds, the lover turns out to be married, and the minister is only human. The Protector then ridicules the Child's pitiful fantasy. Although you feel good about yourself for a little while, idealizing others ultimately further erodes your self-respect.

"I Fell for the Flattery"

Sid worked for Betty, a CEO renowned for her personal power and brilliance. This was his first professional job, and he worked hard, giving extra attention to her pet projects. He was thrilled when Betty picked him as her personal assistant. She praised him for his 24/7 attitude and put down other workers for their lack of ambition. Soon enough, though, Betty found little things to criticize, even when he did well: "You're too bright for a mere A. Work for the A+." She shared private aspects of her life, invited him to her home, and talked about her problems. He quickly learned that she loved being told how fabulous she was and that nothing was ever her fault.

Sid worked extra hours without pay to meet her standards. Friends and coworkers warned that Betty was using him, but he insisted he was learning a lot. Sid's health suffered and his anxiety increased. Betty graded him a "moderate" evaluation, saying she knew he could do better in his time management.

One day, Sid was in a car accident that put him in bed with a shattered leg. When he was released from the hospital, Betty came to his house with an armload of files. "I know you would go crazy not being useful, and besides, we have a deadline." Sid worked to complete the tasks, despite being in constant pain. Betty blew up at him when he was a day late with a report.

This devastated him. Then he realized it felt familiar, and the insight came to him that he was trying to get the praise from Betty that he never got from his parents. They criticized his Bs and never praised his As: "You can do better. Don't be a quitter. Don't complain that the work is hard." They never talked about the difference between "hard" and "abusive." This longing for acceptance also caused him to stay in romantic relationships too long, turning himself into an emotional pretzel to make someone love him. He didn't stop to ask how he honestly felt about his boss or a girlfriend. He was the one who had to prove himself.

It took this extreme episode to see Betty as someone who used people for her own goals. Sid no longer believed she would acknowledge him, and he quit trying to prove to her that he was worthy. This allowed him to stop feeling one-down to her opinions and demands. He stood up to her, demanding a bonus for what he'd accomplished, took two weeks off with pay, and told her it wasn't okay to yell at him. He felt great. Betty turned her charms on another victim when she saw she could no longer control Sid.

He resigned soon after, without anger or fear. "I learned more from this job than I thought! My Child has been 'not good enough' for too long."

Only you can challenge the Child's fear that you'll never be good enough. Believe in yourself, or you will always need others to determine your self-worth.

How Do You Sabotage Intimacy?

We all carry some confusion and shame about past relationships. You'd be unusual if you haven't thrown yourself at someone you idealized or stayed in a situation where you sacrificed your self-respect for the longing of another. These are both ways to sabotage intimacy.

In your younger days, the behavior may have been obvious. Now, it may be more subtle: Do you pretend to have greater intimacy with friends than you feel? Are you as openly sharing with your partner as you'd like? This next exercise will help you gain insight into any current barriers to intimacy.

Self-Discovery Exercise: Should Have, Would Have, Could Have

Recall times when you felt embarrassed and vulnerable after instant intimacy. Did you idealize someone to the point that you sacrificed friends, health, or your money? Recall enmeshed situations where you were miserable and told yourself you couldn't leave. Did you ever figure out why?

In your journal:

Draw three vertical lines down the page, creating three columns. Make the first two just big enough for names. The far right column will hold comments. This exercise will take at least fifteen minutes, although you may want to return to the list, adding names as they occur to you.

Step 1. Think of people whom you have clung to, idealized, or hopelessly tried to please. Include bosses, teachers, ex-partners, family, and coworkers. The central issue is that you feel you should have recognized the problem and done something about it earlier. People who expected special treatment because they were beautiful and talented may come to mind. Include those who were frequently care-less about keeping you waiting or who forgot to repay small loans. Pitiful people who sabotaged themselves, then expected sympathy or bailing out, fit here. Family can certainly be included. Write the names in the first column on the left.

Step 2. In the second column, name the core self that was attracted to each person. Did your Protector like to save them, making you look good or feel needed? Did your Child feel special in their reflected glory? Is it possible that your Adult saw them as damaged, needing another chance, or that your Adult believed they were truly special and deserved to be tolerated? In Sid's case, he soon knew Betty was toxic, but he was caught up in the belief he was learning from a master. More than one self can be involved in each relationship.

Step 3. Ask yourself, "When could I have ended it graciously?" Write your answers in the third column. This is your chance to use hindsight. Be curious and gentle with yourself: "I think I knew from the beginning—he left his wedding ring when he traveled." Alternatively, "She started complaining about two years into the friendship that I wasn't available enough and acted hurt when I spent time with other friends." Include the big stuff: one affair forgiven, followed by another; relationships with addicts (to anything); patho-logical liars; and people who couldn't keep promises.

Step 4. Where are you currently sabotaging intimacy? Be kind to yourself as you name those whom you idealize and think of recent examples of instant intimacy. What do you hope will happen? Let your Child and Adult sort this out, without feeling pressure to change anything right away.

It takes courage to review problems in your past relationships. It takes even more to recognize how you may be continuing with old patterns in the present. There is a big reward for having the courage to trust yourself and be honest with others: deep and lasting rela-tionships that nurture your best self.

It's important to strengthen your intuitive sense about whether an involvement is taking you in a good direction. Some relationships may deserve more time and attention, and others you may want to limit. There may be a few that you recognize it is time to end. This next section offers you a way to view current relationships and will help you define intimacy.

Circles of Belonging

The following model (see figure 1) and exercise will help you identify the levels of belonging you presently have with important people in your life. You'll ask yourself where you would like to invite more intimacy and where you might want to increase some boundaries.

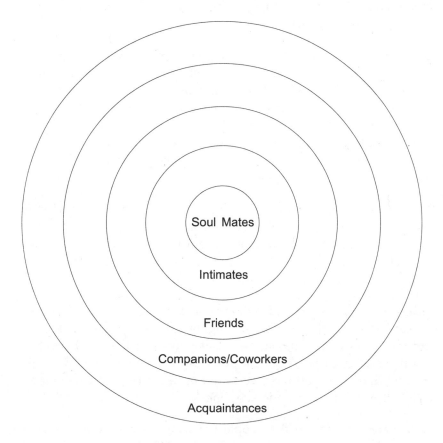

Figure 1: The Circles of Belonging

In this model, everyone who is not currently involved in our life is on the outside. From the moment that people step inside our lives, we arrange them in circles that measure our sense of belonging with them. People we no longer seek out, even if they once were close, are outside.

There are five circles of belonging, starting with the least intimate relationships in the outer circle and becoming increasingly more intimate toward the center. Here's a description of each:

Acquaintances. People you meet more than a few times fit into this outer circle. You may know people for years and enjoy exchanging services with them, but you don't connect with them in other aspects of your life. Acquaintances include people like your mechanic, doctor, and hairdresser. You'd probably offer assistance if something tragic happened to them.

Companions and coworkers. These people have become more than acquaintances as you have worked or studied with them or shared another activity. You seldom go to each other's homes and wouldn't casually reveal the details of your personal problems because you don't know how they'd respond. They are "nice people," but there's no impulse to pursue a deeper relationship. If one of you quits your shared activity or moves away, it's unlikely you'd meet, but you would go to a good-bye party.

Friends. A friend is someone with whom a shared activity is secondary to being together. Friends are the people you tell the personal details of your life. You have a mutual sense of trust and connection. Even if you see older friends infrequently, you make special efforts to support them during troubling times.

Intimates. The people with whom you have a profound sense of empathy are your intimates. Belonging grows with mutual give-and-take. You both feel confident that you can share your feelings and flaws without fear of being pushed away. Even if you disagree or don't like what you hear, you are not likely to reject each other. You talk it through to understanding.

Soul mates. These are the people you can call when you're very upset at three in the morning, and they say, "Come stay with me," or "How much money do you need?" Soul mates are the people we want as romantic partners or as associates in creating a new business, where everything is on the line. Being consistently accepting is the key to this connection, and it cannot be built quickly. To be reflective, nonjudgmental, and honest is hard work and often brings up deep emotional challenges. It is a big responsibility to be this available for more than a couple of people at a time. You can't imagine life without these people. Self-sacrifice is required at times, but it needs to be equal. The intimacy will weaken if sacrifice becomes uneven.

Self-Discovery Exercise: Your Current Circles of Belonging

The intention of this exercise is to help you assess the level of trust and intimacy in current relationships. This exercise may take anywhere from thirty to forty-five minutes, depending on how many people are active in your life. It can be done in stages, adding names as you think of them. Let your Child, Protector, and Adult direct your thoughts. This is private and you don't need to show this to anyone.

In your journal:

You'll need two different colored pencils. Copy the Circles of Belonging from figure 1 as large as you can on one page.

Step 1. Put the names of people you currently spend time with into the circle that feels right for you at this moment. Be sure to include members of your family. Use variations inside the depth of each circle to show levels of belonging within each category.

Step 2. Look over the placement of the names. Do you wish some were deeper toward the center or would you like to move others further out? Allow yourself the freedom to admit a desire for closeness, even if you believe certain people have no time for another friend or you are afraid they may not like you as much as you like them. Draw arrows to show where you would like to move them.

Step 3. Think of where some people in your life might place themselves. Is it different from where you put them? With a different colored pencil, draw an arrow to show where the other person would see themselves. (Example: A coworker loves talking about herself and doesn't notice you are less open. She thinks she's a friend, but you consider her a companion.)

Step 4. Reflect on this process. Are you judging the number of names in each circle, thinking you have too many or too few in some categories? Are you sad at some losses or frustrated with the pressure to be more social with someone than you wish? Where do your life partner and family members belong *at this moment*? Would it surprise them to know you feel this way? Where do you think they would put themselves? Where do you wish they could be?

Natural Fluctuations of Belonging and Intimacy

There will always be movement within your circles of belonging, both inward and away from the center. Life circumstances such as moving away and changing interests will cause fluctuations. There is no point in expecting a relationship to continue if you no longer share similar needs and values with someone. Some friendships fade because one or both people do not have the time it takes to remain close. The love is there, but not the time.

When your trust is betrayed, such as when a painful secret is told or you are deceived, someone can suddenly shift from intimate or friend to being completely outside the circle. This is devastating. What happens next depends on the mutual willingness to rebuild trust or decide to disconnect.

Sometimes when a broken trust is mended, the sense of belonging becomes stronger. Often the memory of the breach will permanently limit how much trust you're willing to risk again. It is your right to decide. The purpose of the exercise you just did is to give you permission to choose whom to trust and how much to trust them. Pretending to trust, or feeling pressure to be closer than feels safe to the Child, will never create real intimacy.

An intimate relationship may shift outward to friend or companion, despite your best efforts. This doesn't mean you have done something wrong. Although it hurts when people reject you, or even if they push you slightly out from their circle of intimates, it's important to support their right to decide whom they trust and how much.

The idea of an ebb and flow in trust feels quite fair and logical to the Adult. However, trying to give the same latitude to family and committed relationships is much harder. In these cases, fluctuations in belonging trigger the fear of rejection.

Preparing for the Next Chapter

It is excruciating when a soul mate, intimate, or family member betrays you. Belonging vanishes and your heart feels broken. Everything may be changed, including your address. Your life will need redirection.

The next chapter focuses on acknowledging your feelings and responding to the needs of your three core selves when you have felt betrayed. You will learn the second foundation trust skill, "Finding Out What You Want," to help return your self-confidence after a break in trust. Betrayal is a powerful experience, regardless of the size of the betrayal or the intention of those who hurt you. Everyone feels knocked down by the confusion and uncertainty that results. Chapter 4 will help you to get back up and decide what you want after trust has been broken.

CHAPTER 4

When You Feel Betrayed

Why do small hurts feel so big?

Betrayal is a very powerful word that is usually reserved for deliberate acts. Trust can also get shaken when we feel we've been rejected or criticized by those who didn't mean to hurt us. This throws us off in our day-to-day interactions and lessens our ability to trust others.

This chapter will help you to understand and cope with your own reactions to feeling betrayed and rejected. We'll return to this topic in chapters 8 and 9, where the focus will be on building your confidence to seek greater intimacy or deciding if it is time to leave.

Everyone has suffered being betrayed. Those who delight in using people may have deceived you. Being rejected by someone you trust is more agonizing. In a normal situation, the trust we have in those we love is more often bruised instead of broken. Yet the feeling of betrayal can be remarkably painful, at least for a while.

If your childhood was marked by severe abuse, it's logical that it would be harder for you to handle small breaks in trust as an adult. The truth is that anyone can have strong reactions to the possibility of being betrayed, even if no abuses occurred in youth.

The slimmest of evidence can evoke the fear that you have been deliberately deceived or rejected. In an instant, you may be overwhelmed by a confusion of feelings, whether or not the trust was broken on purpose. Your core selves split apart and your body gets overpowering signals that something is terribly wrong. You have to struggle against the fears of being rejected and can temporarily lose a sense of reality. This calls out the Protector.

To try to ignore signs of possible betrayal will distract you from clear thinking and is seldom successful. This chapter introduces effective tools to help reclaim your sense of personal power as quickly as possible.

Forms of Betrayal

The four forms of betrayal are *deliberate, careless, unintentional,* and *subconscious.*

- Deliberate betrayals disregard or discount the suffering caused to another person. They are often motivated by self-centered drives, such as greed and revenge.

- Careless betrayals result from self-absorption and a temporary absence of empathy. If asked to put themselves in the other person's place, people who are guilty of careless betrayals will recognize their lapse and feel remorse.

- Unintentional betrayals are often due to misunderstandings. They are also caused by unavoidable circumstances. Sudden illness, cell phone batteries dying, and writing down the wrong date can happen to anyone and prevent the keeping of a promise.

- Subconscious betrayals stem from unacknowledged conflicts that may exist between people or solely within the one who betrays the other person. Hidden resentment or a sense of inadequacy can cause people to break commitments and to not recognize the real reasons for their actions.

Self-Discovery Exercise:
What Does Betrayal Feel Like?

Read the following story and put yourself into the experience. Imagine the stakes are high and you really are counting on this person to the exclusion of others.

> You have an appointment with a specialist for a very personal matter. This meeting is critical to a decision that you have to make right away. Your future rides on what you learn in this meeting. You've spoken with the specialist on the telephone at length. He understands your dilemma, seems genuine in his enthusiasm to help you, and his references are terrific.
>
> You arrive ten minutes early and sit outside the locked office, reviewing your well-prepared notes, trying to be as calm as you can. He doesn't show. You check your cell phone (he has the number), and there are no messages. You check the time, date, and address. You've paid for the appointment in advance, and you were careful to mark your calendar. You call his number and get his answering machine, which says he'll be available later the same day. You check your messages at home, and there are none. Half an hour and then an hour go by. Finally, you give up and leave.

What do you feel? Use a mental form of the Trust Check-In (see chapter 2) as you consider the forms of betrayal below. Let your Child be as irrational and young as it gets. Encourage your Protector to be righteous and angry. Ask your Adult to sit back and wait for a cue. In this way, you can identify where your sensations, emotions, and thoughts run when in the limbo of rejection. Add any feelings you have from similar experiences.

1. What if this were a deliberate betrayal?

The specialist knew you were coming. He just didn't bother to show. Your little problem was of no concern to him, and he feels he earned his fee by the telephone time. He wouldn't have stood you up if you were important. *How do you feel about him? Yourself? What thoughts and memories does this trigger?*

2. What if he were just careless or thoughtless?

He runs toward your car as you pull out of the parking lot. He says he lost track of the time and will meet with you now, but only for half an hour. You take the offered time, and the conversation is scattered. He seems distracted and can't recall the details of your problem. He ends the meeting abruptly, saying "I'm sure you'll do fine. You're very bright." *How does his careless attitude affect you?*

3. Suppose it was unavoidable.

Mistakes and accidents happen. The consultant had written down the time incorrectly and was busy doing research for the meeting he thought was an hour later. He may have had an accident and was unable to reach you. He intended to honor your trust. *What changes occur in your feelings when you learn this?*

4. What if the betrayal were subconscious?

Here is the most difficult issue of betrayal. The consultant didn't intend to stand you up. However, the dilemma you present disturbs him more than he consciously knows. He feels inadequate, or he should be dealing with the issue for himself and is terrified to address it. He loses his appointment book to avoid the pain of exploring it, or he forgets to buy gas and runs out on his way to the appointment. *Where does this take you emotionally?*

In your journal:

Capture any especially strong reactions. Did any of these questions remind you of past events that were painful? If so, please note them. The people who have caused the disappointments and abuse you suffered had their own reasons behind their actions. Unless they explained it to you, there was no way you could know how much or how little it really had to do with you. You can take the sting out of past hurts by sorting the ways they still affect you.

The point of this exercise was for you to grasp that trust may be broken whether it was intentional or not. The specialist not showing up collapses the Child's sense of dependence and throws you into uncertainty. Now we will look at ways to restore your confidence when trust is broken.

How We Use Stories When We Feel Uncertain

We create stories to give us the illusion that we can interpret other people's behavior. Such stories appear in our minds many times each day. It happens when we hear a message with an abrupt tone, or the boss says, "See me after lunch." The purpose is to give us a sense of being in control, often by anticipating worst-case scenarios. Planning a response to possible negative outcomes can be good in some cases. This tendency needs to be explored if you consistently produce feelings of being rejected.

The Child and Protector create stories that produce automatic suspicion and self-doubt. Their intention is to shield you from criticism and betrayal, but these stories are not helpful in building trust in yourself and others. They create suffering and barriers between you and those you love.

None of us can control all our thoughts and feelings. However, you can learn to recognize when you are building a story from your thoughts. The Adult needs to be invited to step in and meet a painful idea with a positive and realistic counter thought. For example, the thought that someone who hasn't called must have forgotten you can evoke the troubling feelings of rejection. Choosing a different story, one where you imagine that the lapse is unintentional, eases the Child's fears and calms the Protector. You can then feel empathy for the other person and cope with the situation in a relaxed and grown-up manner.

Victory over destructive story making begins when you believe you have a choice about the stories you tell yourself. You can see ways to do this by understanding how each of your three core selves handles betrayal.

How the Three Selves Handle Betrayal

Trust is the powerful foundation that supports every aspect of our lives. The three core selves have separate reactions when trust is threatened.

The Child Reacts with Helplessness

The Child has a great deal to lose when friends or loved ones betray you. The fear of loss can plunge the Child into helplessness. What is your first reaction to this list?

- Three close friends go out to dinner and don't invite you.

- A friend offers only a weak "thank you" and barely looks at the gift you made by hand.

- A date greets you at the door with, "Oh, I forgot you were coming."

- Your partner neglects a very important errand, despite your diligence on his or her behalf.

The Child is left holding its feelings all alone. No one asks if you are upset. Imagine five-year-olds facing these disappointments. They would react by pouting and wondering what is wrong with them. Their concern is to hang on to whatever remnants of belonging still exist.

As an adult, you can't call your friends and pout, or berate an ingrate by telling him or her how much care you put into a gift. As for the date that you prepared for, you may never want to go out with them again. The partner issue can leave you feeling sorry for yourself, which is not effective in building trust and intimacy.

You're helpless to do anything with the Child's voice without making yourself feel worse. That's what your Protector is for.

The Protector Leaps to Right and Wrong

The Protector helps the Child escape pain. This older and resourceful self achieves this using anger and self-righteousness and by rejecting those who hurt you.

Getting angry feels good because it counteracts fear and self-pity. In each of the circumstances listed above, the Protector is convinced that the others are clearly wrong. The Protector will list reasons for never seeing any of them again.

Your voice may sound cold when dealing with the people who have hurt you, or you may avoid them if your stress response is freeze or flight. Anger might leak through by neglecting telephone calls or through sarcastic remarks. This hides your pain and prevents more hurt because you stay on the defensive.

The Child's and Protector's manner of handling things leaves the ones who hurt you in charge of addressing the betrayal. An apology may elicit enough warmth to allow reconnection. You might respond by saying, "It's no big deal." Love and intimacy can be bridged over the painful part, but it often leaves a scar that doesn't completely heal.

The Adult Responds to the Whole Story

The Child's and Protector's physical and emotional responses are unmistakable. Your reactions let you know that something might be amiss. The Adult self can then assess the situation from a larger perspective.

A healthy Adult response begins with acknowledging your instinctive reactions and then looks at likely stories to explain them. The Adult's role is to face the fear by admitting your concerns and mistakes, and then asking for honest dialogue. Your Adult self recognizes that this makes you vulnerable to real rejection, but helps you also understand that such openness more often results in increased trust and understanding. Choosing to trust is an essential skill of the Adult self.

The Adult responds to feeling betrayed by considering alternatives, including the possibility that the trust was misplaced. The Adult moderates fears of rejection and possible separation with the faith that honesty and compassion will produce healthy results.

Overcoming Uncertainty

You deserve to feel certain of where you stand with someone you care about. There is a dread of possible betrayal if you don't know where you stand with each other. Conversation is stilted between you so that you won't reveal anything that could lead to rejection. This causes both people to be guarded.

The first test after someone hurts you is to dispel the doubts that limit your confidence in what feels real. Do this by asking to hear the explanation of the other. Listen with respect and feel what resonates.

Challenging Uncertainty After Betrayal

"If I can *understand* it, I can *stand* it," will help you survive the uncertainty caused by upsets. Ask yourself if the action feels deliberate, careless, unintentional, or subconscious. It may be just one of the above, but often it feels like a mixture. Asking this question begins your Adult's entry onto the scene.

Listen to what the other person has to say after an emotional storm has quieted. Ask real questions. Listen carefully to the story you are told. It might be the truth or a variation of the truth. If you are not convinced, what feelings are coming through that make you doubt the story?

Whether or not you trust the answer depends on how it matches with your own experience. Put the relationship on hold for a while, so you can assess the situation from an Adult viewpoint. Take time alone and do the following exercise.

Self-Discovery Exercise:
Asking Your Adult to Assess a Betrayal

This exercise gives your Adult a chance to practice looking at a betrayal without having to act. It will help you understand what you think and believe after a betrayal, and it will make you more aware of the feelings and doubts that limit your ability to trust.

In your journal:

Choose an issue that has affected your trust with someone important to you. Practice on a small, recent event. Afterward, you can look at older, larger betrayals.

If you choose a betrayal that happened when you were a child, note how little you could have understood at the time. What has your Adult learned since then?

Write down the name of the betrayer and the specific betrayal. State what form you think the betrayal took, and then write your responses to each of the following questions. Note the emotions and physical sensations that arise.

- How did the other person justify what was done to you?

- What did you believe was his or her excuse?

- What else was going on that you weren't told about or that you wanted to know?

- Did this person do this only to you? Were there selfish or cruel acts against others?

- Have you ever done anything like this to the other person or to anyone? What is your story about that?

- What stopped you from seeing this coming?

- Did you do anything to deserve being treated this way?

- Do you believe you were responsible in any way? Were you told it was your fault?

- Should you quit the relationship?

- What does this betrayal remind you of? Name other times, people, and betrayals that come to mind.

Do a brief Trust Check-In to see how your Child and Protector are responding to the betrayals. If they're feeling a little shaken, gently remind them that you are not taking any actions, just remembering. Take a walk or call a friend.

The following excerpt from a story that appeared in the *San Francisco Chronicle* demonstrates the power our early experiences continue to have over us:

> The husband of a woman I once knew committed suicide in his early forties. Afterward, the woman and her two young, now fatherless children endured a kind of exile.

They hadn't died, but essential supports fell away. Even some close family members pulled back, fearing that if they extended the usual kindness and invitations to Thanksgiving dinner they would be called upon to carry a much heavier burden—to offer financial help, for example. In time, the diminished family of three wove a new social web composed of some loyalists from the past and some gradually acquired new friends. Back in the city after years in the suburbs, the widow trained herself for a different career and flourished in it. She remarried, happily. The kids went to good schools, where they excelled.

The woman's son, now a middle-aged man with children of his own, told me that those childhood years in the wilderness of the socially cutoff had left him forever wary. He's slow to invest fully in a new friendship, and hypersensitive to slights, real and imagined. A friend's inattention or silence always conjures his childhood time of sudden, devastating, inexplicable loss and rejection. When you've been treated like a pariah, it's hard not to feel like one. You never stop sensing that the seemingly solid ground you walk on may at any time split open without warning. (Leider 2003, 68)

It might be tempting to stay in the role of innocent victim, but that leaves you unable to trust anyone very deeply. You can change your relationship to your past by adopting new habits and skills that support the wisdom and compassion you want to experience.

The next step is to see new options and express the truth as you see it. This gives you the power to know what you want. Only then can you share your needs and dreams with those whom you choose to trust.

Knowing What You Want

You have an innate sense of knowing what you want. Telling others what you want and listening to what they want forms the basis for deep and lasting relationships. You can begin the process by considering what you don't want. The trail of broken trusts holds lots of good information, and each day brings new ideas.

Avoid Blocking Intimacy

We create a major block to intimacy when we tell ourselves that we already know what the other person will say. This stops us from considering what we want. We soon forget how important discussing what you want is to maintaining any relationship.

Think about what isn't working for you and focus on what you want to try. We often wait until a relationship is at its breaking point. When someone demands, "What *do* you want?" it doesn't invite our best response. Most of us feel our minds go blank or are overcome with anger, which blocks a coherent answer.

The following foundation skill will encourage you to discover what you want to change in a relationship after you have felt betrayed. This process is inspired by the work of John Gray (1994) and Laurel Mellin (2003). Repeat this with as many people and incidents as you wish. The more you do, the more efficient you'll become in knowing what you want.

Second Foundation Skill: Finding Out What You Want

Practice on a recent event when your Child was stuck in helplessness or your Protector couldn't let go of being right. Working on a recent hurt can produce insights about your past. An example is at the end, so read all the way through to calm your Child's fears.

In your journal:

Write a short letter to a person about a current issue of betrayal that upsets you. If you don't have one right now, choose an issue that bothered you recently. Don't choose the worst event in your life, at least not yet. This letter will not be sent, so be as outrageous as you need to be. Allow all the feelings out of your body and onto the page. Don't judge any thoughts or worry about sentence structure.

Complete each sentence with spontaneous, emotional language. Answer in whatever order you prefer, going back and forth between the questions as different emotions arise. This should take about twenty minutes to complete and should be done in one sitting. (Write by hand instead of using the computer, at least the first few times you do this exercise.)

Dear _____ , *I am writing this letter to tell you how I feel about* _____ *(drinking too much at my birthday; not returning my calls; not giving me the raise you'd promised).*

I am angry that you _____ . (Keep the words simple so that a child can relate to it; express "stuck" feelings of hate; call the person names; make "you" statements.)

I am upset that _____ . (Be straightforward with no apology or effort to understand or forgive.)

I am scared that _____ . (Include your fears about bringing up this topic and the consequences of telling your feelings; explore any fears that may have played into the scene.)

I feel guilty that _____ . (Acknowledge your part in the relationship. Perhaps you feel sorry for the pain that the other person experiences in his or her life. This is to recall compassion for another's suffering, regardless of the cause.)

This reminds me of _____ . (Let the feelings bring back memories of being treated in a similar way. This is the most important realization and can help you separate the present from a painful past.)

What I want to happen is _____ . (Ask for what you wished had happened, and what you want from the other, to begin healing the relationship or to end it. Don't block anger and other feelings as they come up. Ask for what you want even if you don't believe it's possible.)

What I appreciate about you is _____ . (This might be only, "Thank you for reading this." It can also be a remembrance of how much you appreciate specific qualities the other person has.)

Your signature _____ . (Sign it however you want.)

Here is an example: Two friends formed a walking club and didn't invite you to join. Your "Finding Out What You Want" letter might read as follows.

Dear Friends,

I am so angry that you excluded me. You had to have talked about me and decided I wasn't acceptable. How would you feel if I did the same? Which I never would because I am a nice person.

To say I am hurt is too small. This exclusion cuts me deeply. I've tried too hard to be good friends with each of you, and now I feel like I've lost two friends at once. My heart is broken.

I'm afraid something is wrong with me. This brings up all my feelings of not being chosen for teams, and being so lonely growing up—the oddball who studied all the time and wasn't popular. I feel scared that you didn't want to include me. I don't know what to do.

I don't feel guilty, but I guess I'm sorry that I am so battered by this I can't even call one of you and ask what is wrong. I'm sorry you didn't think you were important enough to me that I'd care. I know you're good people, but . . .

It reminds me of my childhood. I felt this a lot with my father always choosing my brother to spend time with him, not including me.

What do I want? I'd like an apology or explanation from you. You've not contacted me about anything since last week, and I want you to be my friends. I want to find out if there's anything I've done to deserve exclusion. I'd also like to be strong enough to allow people to get together without my involvement without me feeling wretched about myself. I want to feel okay and for you to feel good, too. This is not the end of the world, and if for some reason I have ignored signals from you, I want to learn them. I will survive.

What I appreciate: You are strong and honest people. I feel now that I can approach you with this. You'll be honest with me and I can tell you how I feel and what I want. If this is the end of our relationship, I want to think of the good times, and how much I love and admire you both.

xoxo, Me

Working through negative stories of feeling betrayed helps clarify your authentic feelings and needs. It is often the case that there is no intention to reject you. For example, the two friends from this example might have needed privacy to talk over a personnel problem at their business. Still, every time you acknowledge hurt feelings and release the pain, you increase your ability to cope whenever you feel betrayed.

Preparing for the Next Chapter

It can be just as devastating to realize you've hurt someone as it is to feel betrayed by another. The next chapter will give you new ways to view how you can betray someone you love. The exercises from chapter 5 can be used to help you sort through the healthy guilt and old shame that could be limiting your self-worth.

Practice the exercises and questions from chapter 4 as new issues come up. Your ability to be trustworthy increases when you improve your skills in understanding betrayal by others.

How You Can Betray Another

How can I mend a break in trust?

This chapter will help you sort out what happens when you have betrayed someone you care about. When you feel betrayed, your response is based on your history and the stories you tell yourself. When you betray others, you observe the betrayal from a different perspective.

Guilt is a powerful teacher but a terrible master. You can become more trustworthy by studying how you have hurt others. Some forms of betrayal will be painfully familiar, while others may be only in your past. Practice compassion for yourself as you explore this difficult topic.

How We Can Hurt and Betray Others

This chapter will explore four different forms of betrayal:

- passive dishonesty and avoiding conflict
- unintended and misinterpreted actions

- impulsive and thoughtless acts

- deliberate deceit and acts of revenge

Passive Dishonesty and Avoiding Conflict

If you think people will get mad if you're honest, you may withhold how you feel. Withholding is as damaging to trust as deliberate betrayal. Not stating your needs is a passive form of dishonesty.

We tell ourselves we can't bear to bring up a difficult subject with another. This leads to acting out in hurtful ways. Do any of the following behaviors feel familiar?

- claiming to be "just teasing," when you bring up a sensitive subject in an offhand way

- responding to a request with resentful sarcasm, then insisting you didn't mean anything

- trespassing personal boundaries, like reading mail because you "have a right to know"

- lying by omission, justified because you don't want to make the other person angry

- trying to get what you want by dropping hints

- announcing what someone is feeling without proof: "I know you're angry."

Sometimes a "white lie" pops out. This is the Protector keeping the Child from getting in trouble. Your Adult needs to admit your responsibility as soon as it's aware of the deceit. It takes courage to tell the whole story. The betrayal becomes deliberate when, to hide your feelings, you claim someone is being too sensitive. To avoid confrontation, you make someone else suffer in uncertainty. The betrayal often happens so fast, no one is sure what is real.

"What Was I Supposed to Say?"

Bill and Connie were curled up on the couch, relaxed and loving as they celebrated their tenth wedding anniversary. Bill was talking about how they had changed. He chuckled and patted Connie's leg, saying, "I get three more pounds every year of my wife to love."

A pain exploded in Connie's chest. All the loving energy vanished as she leapt from the couch. She told herself he couldn't be so insensitive if he really loved her. Connie's eyes went big with disbelief. "I've carried your three children and developed thyroid problems as a result. All you notice is how fat I am?"

"I can't believe I married you," she continued. "You're a selfish monster! You've done this one too many times. How could I ever think you loved me?"

Bill sat upright on the couch. "What's wrong? I didn't mean anything by that. I was just teasing. You're always complaining about your weight, and you know I don't mind!"

Connie saw before her a liar or a stranger. Bill couldn't pretend he didn't know his words would hurt her. She burst into tears and Bill got up and held her. He told her how sorry he was. She pretended to accept his apology for "teasing." Both acted contrite and tried to make the best of the evening.

Bill's use of sarcasm ruined his chance to talk about his real concerns about Connie's weight and health. By pretending it was just a misunderstanding, Connie didn't have to confront Bill's unhappiness with her size. These two need to become more honest, and Connie has to face any feelings *she* has about her weight, or the memory of the event will fester and explode again.

Self-Discovery Exercise:
Are You Passively Dishonest?

This is a chance to review your style of dealing with sensitive issues. Be gentle with yourself as you acknowledge the ways you may not be honest with others.

In your journal:

Writing down your responses helps to highlight a pattern of passive dishonesty. Consider the following questions, noting the people you have treated in each way. Ask yourself why you might do this. Make a note about how the Child and Protector influence each one.

- Do you use teasing or sarcasm rather than saying what is bothering you?

- Do you overrehearse before asking for something, as if preparing for rejection?

- When you are upset with someone's habits, do you drop hints rather than asking for change?

- Do you complain about friends, a boss, or partner, but you wouldn't dare to talk directly to them?

- Do you blame others' moods for your unwillingness to confront conflicts?

- Do you hide your "guilty pleasures" (shopping, reading magazines, computer games) believing your partner makes you feel like a naughty child?

- Have you recently denied or hidden a binge, a mistake, or a feeling of being ashamed?

Recall earlier times as you write the names of the people you have hurt and betrayed and recognize which of your selves are involved. Were these behaviors how you experienced freedom when you were a child? Did you observe these patterns in your family, and now they've become habits that you'd like to change? Note any thoughts arising from your Adult about how you could change them and where you might want to start.

Unintended and Misinterpreted Actions

We've all had the experience of hurting someone when we meant no harm. In an instant, a relationship can change from friendship to being mere acquaintances. Those who are hurt can be so distrustful that they may not feel safe to talk it over. Yet very few people can brush off a friend or loved one's anger. We want those we've hurt to know we take them seriously, even if we feel they're being unfair or extreme in their reaction.

Protesting your innocence can lead to blame instead of understanding. The following self-discovery exercise will help you track your responses to this awkward experience.

Self-Discovery Exercise: How Do You React When You Are Accused?

This exercise will help expose your reactions when someone has accused you of being insensitive. Read the following scenario and answer the questions at the end as if you were the person in this situation:

Your friend lost his job six months ago due to downsizing, and unemployment compensation is not covering his bills. You have a good job and can afford to help. He is afraid of losing his car and accepts your offer to cover the monthly payments. You mean it when you tell him not to worry about paying it back until he is working again. When a mutual friend expresses concern about your friend's situation, you tell him about the loan.

Your friend learns about the conversation and leaves an angry message on your answering machine. He accuses you of betraying his trust and making him look pitiful. He has not shared his financial stress with anyone except you, "and now everyone knows I'm a loser!" He promises to seek a high-interest loan to pay you back.

In your journal:

Writing down your responses will help you get clear about your feelings. Imagine you experienced this incident, or perhaps recall a real experience when told you were indiscreet.

- How does your body react upon hearing about your friend's anger at this felt betrayal?

- What does your own hurt Child feel?

- How does your Protector respond to your friend's accusations?

- Consider the situation from your friend's point of view. How would you justify the hurt and sense of betrayal?

Impulsive and Thoughtless Acts

Impulsive actions spring from the Child's exuberance. They are also the Protector's way of avoiding trouble. You feel foolish upon being found out and want to believe you will never do it again. This may reveal a compulsion that won't be easy to quit.

Here is a simple rule to test if you have been acting from childish motives. Ask yourself, "How would I feel if someone at the same level of intimacy did to me what I am doing to them?" Familiar examples include

- flattering someone's appearance, then making a little joke about it behind the person's back

- forgetting or not attending an important event, then telling a white lie to cover up

- looking into someone's bathroom cabinet, trying perfumes or examining the medications

- letting sexual energy go too far while dancing with a friend's spouse

- passing along gossip about someone you know, then worrying your friend will find out

- using someone's property without asking, then saying "I thought it was okay"

These examples point to the Child's natural curiosity and desire to be special. Continuing this behavior will undermine your self-trust. It becomes a deliberate betrayal once you acknowledge that it isn't as harmless as you'd told yourself. Expanding your self-confidence will help you restrain these impulses and instill the pride of being a trustworthy adult.

Deliberate Deceit and Acts of Revenge

Anyone under enough stress can be susceptible to acting against his or her own morals and rules. Once it happens, the Child can become terrified of disaster. The Protector engages in lies and cover-ups, and acts out increasingly complicated forms of betrayal to appease the Child.

Your Adult self may not register what you are doing until you are caught. The Adult awakens to the chaos with the question, "How could I have done that?"

What Causes Us to Betray Others?

People with deep unmet needs for belonging often seek revenge on those who hurt them. Rejection or disrespect can push them over the edge. The power of these impulses reveals how profoundly they are split inside. The Child and Protector are in control when

- A minor betrayal gives you permission to hurt someone back even more.

- Feeling abandoned justifies repeated calls to hear an ex-lover's voice and then hanging up.

- Stalking counters the agony of jealousy.

- The influence of drugs or alcohol helps rationalize impetuous acts.

The Adult has failed to control the inner rage and desperation. The underlying reasons for betrayal reveal the insecurity of the Child. Betrayal that stems from a desire for revenge is the work of the Protector.

Deceit is the last straw for many relationships. Deceit can also be the ultimate cry for help in the case of addiction or other compulsive behavior. The absence of a healthy Adult leaves the Child to repeat the behavior until stopped. There seems no way out of this cycle.

The antidote for this level of acting out is a complete examination of your personal life and choices. This is followed by climbing out of self-hate and despair, and coping with guilt. It takes immense courage, as you will see in the story below.

"Deceiving Myself Betrayed Others"

Lana had been in a committed partnership with Nora for ten years when she registered for graduate school. Lana's student loans and fewer work hours *created a financial strain, but Nora was willing to work overtime and reduce expenses, even vacations and eating out, in order to support the two of them. After the first semester, Nora found a credit card statement in Lana's name while recycling office papers. It was addressed to a private post office box; the bill had reached the credit limit of $5,000. Nora confronted Lana with the statement, comparing this secrecy to infidelity. Lana reacted angrily. "I'll pay it off when I get my degree. I can't live under the pressure of feeling so poor!"*

Lana insisted she was justified in this small freedom. Nora couldn't believe Lana didn't understand it was a betrayal of their trust. When Nora demanded that she cut up the credit card, Lana began to sob. This level of distress worried them, and Lana agreed to meet alone with a therapist.

There she admitted that she spent the money on frivolous things, "but without it, I'd feel trapped. It makes me feel safe." Lana described a childhood of neglect. "My mother was depressed and on heavy medication. I was left crying for hours in my crib and my five-year-old brother fed me peanut butter and applesauce. My mother died when I was thirteen. I've worked for years on forgiving my parents for not taking care of me."

What Lana hadn't yet explored was her inability to trust anyone. Lana had learned too early she couldn't count on others to meet her needs. As a young girl, she hid candy and took loose change from her father's dresser to buy more. Lana became a compulsive overeater, then managed her weight in adolescence with bulimia and starving. She later traded this compulsion for alcohol and drugs, managing to avoid severe addiction.

As a young adult, she reveled in living on her own, including spending money with abandon. This gave her a sense of fullness. "I'd sometimes buy things for the thrill, returning them the next day." She let bills go unpaid and avoided collection agencies by moving. Lana borrowed money from family members and ignored the debts. "They all have more than I do."

In therapy, Lana acknowledged the old resentments she still carried. She linked her early neglect with the need to meet emotional needs in any way she could. Lana's Child self had learned to equate security with meeting every whim, without regarding the consequences. She was shocked at her denial over the credit card issue. "How could I not have seen that I betrayed Nora?" The resulting guilt and shame was forcing a change.

This breakdown in denial gave her incentive to address her betrayal of others. She made a list of all her debts and was stunned to find it amounted to over $15,000. Her first act of trust was to tell her partner the whole story *and reveal the list. With Nora's understanding and support, she contacted each member of her family, citing plans to repay them. Her sister was delighted and told her how much her honesty meant. Her brother forgave the debt; he was just glad to be in contact again. Lana realized how her denial and resentment had prevented her from being close with them. "I can't believe how long this has been eating at my ability to trust myself and others. It's worth everything it costs to repay it all." She cut up the credit card. "This time I loved doing it! I felt free."*

Deep fears and unmet needs often are at the root of compulsive sexual infidelity, addictive spending, and secret abuse of drugs or alcohol. Other people may focus on why you continue to break your promises, not understanding the compulsion isn't about hurting them. Lying is the deliberate betrayal. Intimacy and trust can never be built on active dishonesty.

When You Are Ready to Heal

It's freeing to acknowledge when we have betrayed others and want to stop. However, many cling to a conviction that they did a bad thing, which must prove they are unlovable. This is called *shame*. Shame prevents us from opening our hearts to those we've hurt. It keeps us from learning from our mistakes and imprisons us in despair. We remain helpless when we believe that our past defines us.

The first step in healing these patterns is to acknowledge that you have a problem and want to stop. The next step is to seek help from self-help groups or professionals who will treat you with compassion and give solid support.

You can do a great deal of the healing before facing anyone you have wronged. That choice comes later, when you are strong enough to hear their story. Everyone bears some guilt and regrets. It is proof that you are merely human, not evidence that you are a bad person pretending to be good.

This next section has ideas about how you can move beyond guilt and shame and increase your trustworthiness along the way. These methods can move you out of the darkness of shame into honesty with yourself and others.

Undoing the Damage

Your self-worth should not be measured only by how often you have broken a trust or betrayed those you love. Real self-worth increases when you learn from your mistakes and give tender regard to others who feel betrayed by you. It matters less what form of betrayal it is than how well you handle the aftermath of confusion and hurt. Careless and unintentional actions often will appear deliberate until you explain and try to understand the effect your lapse has had on the other person.

By supporting others in their healing after you've hurt them, you will reduce your own guilt and increase the chances of regaining lost trust. Here are some suggestions on how to assist others in regaining their self-trust. They are accompanied by self-discovery exercises to increase your empathy and empower your Adult.

Accept Others' Need for Space

People who feel betrayed often need to break off contact for a time. Your Child desperately wants to apologize and quickly explain away the problem. The panic you feel is about whether you'll be reinstated into the circles of belonging again. Healthy guilt can drive you to seek self-awareness and guidance from others. Shame makes you so self-absorbed that you may ignore important boundaries, such as by constantly e-mailing or calling. The best rule is to give the other person the time off that he or she requests.

Basic Rules for Giving Time

Those who have been hurt need to be in control. Arrange with them whatever time they need to wait until it feels safe to talk again. They may need to avoid you for a day or much longer. Saying they are "being unfair" will only add weight to the betrayal. Your need to be understood is less important than their right to feel safe.

The compulsion to give excuses comes from the Protector. Your Adult needs to take responsibility for your actions. Use the second foundation skill, Finding Out What You Want (see chapter 4), to discover what you want, to calm your younger self, and to acknowledge the fact that you've been rejected.

Self-Discovery Exercise: Establishing a "Safety Zone"

We must each find our own way to cope before we can discuss what happened. The ones who feel betrayed need a "safety zone" to restore confidence to speak from their Adult selves. The ones who feel guilty can use this time to regain honesty with themselves and to prepare to listen without becoming defensive.

This exercise focuses on your own experience of needing space after being hurt. Each of us has different needs, and you can build empathy by exploring what works for you. Set aside about thirty minutes. There are examples after each step, so read through the entire exercise before starting.

In your journal:

Step 1. Recall a few events over the years where you felt betrayed or your boundaries were invaded. Include any events you remember, regardless of magnitude. Note a name and quick phrase to remind you of each one. Recall whether you wanted to talk immediately afterward, or the number of days before you knew what you wanted to say. How long do you *wish* you had waited and why?

Example 1: *R borrowed my car, returned it late, trashed and on empty. R wanted to talk, but I was too angry and waited three days while I self-righteously cleaned it myself. It was too many days, because R wanted to make it right. The car is just a possession, and both our childish behaviors compromised the friendship. My Protector didn't want to listen to R's excuses.*

Example 2: *M promised to repay a loan, but kept delaying. She sent me an e-mail a week after the deadline, saying she only had half together and asking what I wanted her to do. I sent a scathing reply, with a list of her flaky habits. It triggered an e-mailed avalanche of stored irritations on both sides. I wish I had waited a day at least, and talked it over in person or by telephone. E-mail is way too instantaneous!*

Step 2. Imagine if the other person in each scenario had sent a note offering space and time from the Adult's perspective. Note the sentiments that would have made *you* feel safe and respected.

Imaginary note from R (left in mailbox or e-mailed): *I blew it with the car. Excuses are available upon request. You are important to me, and I promise I will listen to what you have to say, even if you yell. I want to make it right with the car, including an excellent detailing job, but don't want to invade your space until you are ready to see my sorry face.*

Imaginary response from M: *Your e-mail hurt, but guess I deserved it. I understand your anger with me, and am working nonstop to get the money together. I'll drop what I have together in the mail today, and will continue until it is all paid back. I appreciate the loan. I'd like to earn your trust back, but know it can't happen overnight. It's your call. Let me know if we can talk on the telephone or in person.*

Step 3. Consider past situations where you were the one who blew it. Disregard any judgments in how the other person handled it at the time. In your journal, write a note to them about each incident. Offer them space and acknowledge your role. Make sure it removes the pressure to be nice. The note works best if short, clear, and not about your needs.

Take 100 Percent of the Responsibility

It may seem counterintuitive to build honesty and trust by taking 100 percent of the responsibility for what happened. The logic is in the application. Taking responsibility frees you from shame and helplessness, and you can focus on resolving problems that you can do something about.

Examine your own intentions and behavior whenever you have been involved in a betrayal. You don't have to figure out other people's psychological issues. It's a big enough job to do it for yourself, and greatly simplifies the healing that can be done. You may learn to enjoy not having to be right all the time, and this speeds up the healing process.

Self-Discovery Exercise:
The Joy of Being Wrong

This exercise is a way to dispel much of the confusion created when you are defensive. The goal is to embrace how *right* other people are in what they believe. Switch places to experience an upsetting incident from another's point of view.

Read through the entire process before starting. The exercise should take no more than thirty minutes and is best done all at once.

In your journal:

Step 1. Recall and note an incident where you acted badly by your own definition. Note what you did, and how you tried to minimize it. Did you make a quick apology and move on but not really resolve anything? Did you end up feeling so guilty that the other person had to take care of you? Did you deny the other person's hurt feelings as being silly or "too sensitive"?

Examples:

- I teased my child in front of her friends.

- I laughed at a coworker, later realizing I'd probably hurt his feelings.

- I revealed a secret about a friend, and she found out.

- I forgot a task that made my spouse's day difficult, then blamed him for not reminding me.

- I flirted with a cute girl, then denied it was a big deal when my girlfriend got mad.

Step 2. Close your eyes and step into the experience as if it were a dream. See the experience from the betrayed person's perspective: sit where the other person sat, be in the other person's body, and feel his or her hurt. Listen to yourself from that perspective. Let your empathy grow as you invite that person's discomforts to rise up. Trace any pain by placing your hands on your body where you sense it. What would that person's Child be feeling? How might the Protector want to numb his or her pain? Avoid making excuses for the incident that started this.

Step 3. Write down how wrong *you* were to act that way from the other person's viewpoint. Use whatever words come to mind. Ask from the other's perspective, "What do I want to hear from the one who hurt me?"

Step 4. Take your original position and imagine saying to the person you hurt, "I'm very sorry. I was lost in myself and acted badly toward you. You didn't deserve it. You are absolutely right. I am totally wrong. What do you need from me to know that I understand and am sorry that I hurt you?"

Warning: It is meaningless to say, "I'm sorry if you *felt* I was . . ." even in fantasy. You either validate the other person's perceptions, or you don't. The joy comes when you find that you can survive being wrong, and that the other person can feel good about you. The cycle of hurt and blame is stopped.

Step 5. Move back into the position of the one who felt betrayed. How would it feel to hear these words of acknowledgment, rather than defensive remarks? What would you ask for? What would you need to let go of the pain? Write down any brilliant ideas and save them for the next time you hurt someone and need to apologize.

Should You Tell?

Your first consideration in answering this question is the well-being of others involved. Would it cause more problems if you confess to something the other person doesn't know about? Talk it over with a discreet friend or counselor. Honest discussions can help you explore your motivation for the betrayal and help you decide whether to share it and how you might cope with the aftermath.

If you choose to speak to the one you have betrayed, the other person is not obligated to listen. Admitting your carelessness and offering amends can help you feel better. However, apologizing does not mean you'll automatically be forgiven. A break in trust can't be healed simply because you feel bad and are committed to changing your behavior.

Rebuilding Lost Trust and Intimacy

No process can guarantee forgiveness or the regaining of lost intimacy, but acknowledging and listening can encourage such miracles.

Those who feel betrayed will control how much lost trust and intimacy can be rebuilt. Even if the break in trust seemed minor to you, it may have recalled a much bigger betrayal from the other person's past, one that he or she cannot easily release.

Some people appear to be forgiving, but won't participate at the level you need to feel trusting and trusted. Observe how those who feel betrayed work through the aftermath. You took responsibility, gave them space, and made the amends they requested. That doesn't mean they'll ever trust you again. Accepting their rejection is the last amend you need to make.

Betraying others is a part of being human. Accepting it as a universal experience can help you accept your guilt and have compassion for your own suffering. It's never easy to "just let it go." Keep using the processes in this book, and you'll soon be able to accept your mistakes as a necessary part of reclaiming your authentic self.

Preparing for the Next Chapter

The next chapter identifies your own habits and attitudes that hurt you. You'll have the opportunity to change old beliefs and make new commitments to yourself. Learning when it is necessary to put yourself first increases your self-trust and gives you the confidence to embrace the future.

CHAPTER 6

How You Can
Betray Yourself

Why do I break so many promises to myself?

The person you need to trust first is yourself. No one can be as consistently supportive of you as you can learn to be. Being kind to yourself increases self-confidence and lessens your need for approval. Loving and caring for yourself not only increases self-trust, it also deepens your connection with others.

You can build self-esteem by focusing on meeting your own needs first. Many try to practice this but are afraid of being seen as selfish. In fact, self-reliant people have the patience and energy to support those they care about.

This chapter will help you recognize the habits and beliefs that undermine your efforts to achieve self-reliance. From there, you can choose new behaviors that will increase your emotional resiliency and self-esteem.

How Well Do You Treat Yourself?

Try this quick assessment of how well you treat yourself. Do you

- tend to break resolutions that would make you healthier and happier?

- delay your own plans for the convenience of other people?

- worry about problems more than you actively seek solutions?

- talk negatively to and about yourself?

- keep adding to your "to do" list, but don't reduce expectations in other areas?

- spend your money carelessly?

- endanger yourself through a self-destructive habit?

- delay getting emotional or medical help until in crisis?

- procrastinate to the point that it creates chaos in your life or work?

- dwell on your mistakes and judge yourself more harshly than you would a friend?

A yes answer to these questions shows low self-reliance. When you do these things, you are breaking promises to yourself and ignoring your needs. Friends would feel betrayed if you treated them the same way. You can decide to become a better friend to yourself. Learning to like and care for yourself may be the most important step to take in your journey to deep and lasting relationships with others.

Forms of Self-Betrayal

Some common traps that undermine self-trust and confidence are believing you are flawed; being overly responsible; low self-esteem appearing as self-doubt; and self-destructive habits.

Believing You Are Flawed

Most people struggle at times with the fear that there is something deeply flawed within them. Recognizing this is a common belief doesn't mean it disappears, but the fear does begin to fade once you confront it.

You no longer need to think of yourself as a bad person struggling to be good. Your Adult self has probably tried to cast off your self-criticism many times. Yet whenever you make a mistake, you see how much of your impossible expectations still hang on. It is easy to recognize by the sudden reemergence of hateful self-talk from the Protector.

Adults who grew up with constant criticism often believed they deserved it. Their Protectors continue to exaggerate perceived faults and minimize good qualities. These adults may seek out or tolerate people who berate them. And even those who had a mixture of praise and criticism can still hold some concerns about not being as wonderful as they should be.

Consider how it might have been if your parents and teachers had always encouraged you to do these things:

- Love yourself and others for our innate goodness.

- Acknowledge yourself for who you are and what you *can* do.

- Dream big dreams, and know that failure is only possible if you don't try.

- Have confidence in your abilities and learn from your mistakes.

- Like the way you look and learn ways to enhance your beauty.

- Do things in your own style and try new ideas.

- Trust your instincts, feelings, and observations.

- Refuse to tolerate abuse of any kind from anyone.

How do you feel reading this list? If you feel sad, be gentle with yourself. You can learn to encourage yourself in just these ways. The following exercise looks at the early experiences that may have stopped you from accepting yourself as you are. Doing this exercise can relieve the self-hate that has demoralized you for years.

Self-Discovery Exercise:
When Did You First Try to Be Perfect?

In this writing exercise, you'll explore the first time you wanted to be perfect, how it felt, and what you learned from it. This exercise will take up to fifteen minutes. Write for as long or as short a time as you wish.

In your journal:

Step 1. Recall your earliest memory of believing you were imperfect. Use these questions to write a brief summary: Who made you feel that way and how? What did you do to try to be "good enough" afterward? Did you throw yourself into the task? With what success? Did you decide you were a hopeless case? What did that produce in you? What can you see as an adult that you couldn't understand at the time?

Bill's example: *I was the youngest of six children, and my elderly parents had no time for me. I idolized my brother, who was older by six years, and tried to be just like him. I guess it was awkward having a little kid follow-ing him around when he was adjusting to being a teen. He told me I was retarded and to stop hanging around. I was crushed and decided I must be stupid, so I stopped trying to be a good kid. I settled for C grades, started smoking cigarettes at age ten, and said I didn't care about my future. I feel sad that I focused on the message that I was weird and unwanted. I can see now that I also got the same message from my parents. Teachers and other kids around me tried to reach out and help. It's hard now not to think I was stupid for believing it. I also recognize that I wanted to be great, and that's what made me choose my cool brother to copy.*

Step 2. Write a letter to your younger self. Use language that makes sense to the age of your Child. Explain and commiserate with him or her about feeling imperfect. Recall what was terrific about you at that age. What good qualities did you fail to recognize or did you hide away from critical eyes? Were you embarrassed about being noticed for admirable qualities? This letter exults in the unique human being you were then and are still.

Perfectionism is a habit your Child learned in self-defense. The cost of this habit is the freedom to let things unfold in their own time. We feel panic when things don't go as we planned and irritation when others don't do what we want. Trying to be perfect separates us from those we love. Lose the need to be right, and you gain the right to be loved.

Being Overly Responsible

The fear of being considered selfish can push us into enmeshment. Those who sacrifice their own happiness for the needs of others suffocate their own self-expression. This results in resentment toward those you help while you can't see a way out of taking care of them.

Exuberance and self-interest are born into every one of us. The following experiences destroy these natural instincts by making a child overly responsible:

- parents who were helpless due to illness or addiction

- denial of hobbies or new clothes because they limited your siblings' or parents' wants

- pressure to be constantly useful: "Mommy needs you. You don't have time to play"

- abuse by caretakers, who then were self-absorbed in guilt or blamed you

Growing up like this teaches children to be overly responsible and to tolerate adult levels of stress. Surviving these experiences is an achievement. You may require therapy or group support to reject the aftermath of shame and unhealthy guilt. Overly responsible adults can feel like children pretending to be grown-ups, despite their competence, as the following story illustrates.

"I Was Pretending to Be an Adult"

When Jeff was twenty-four, he sought hypnotherapy to overcome an odd phobia: he couldn't sign his name in front of anyone. He had recently been promoted to manager of his department in a manufacturing firm. He had to sign for deliveries, and he created a logjam by insisting on reviewing each one alone in his office. He was too ashamed to admit his phobia and knew he'd soon have to quit, or he would be fired.

At his initial hypnotherapy session, the therapist explained that a phobia is often caused by an early, traumatic experience. By finding the original event, his present fear could be eliminated. Jeff closed his eyes and began to relax. He drifted back to when he learned to be afraid of signing his name, and he recalled how he hid this in previous jobs, high school, and grade school.

Suddenly he saw himself at eight years old in a department store. He was laboriously filling out a check with people staring at him. "I can't believe I forgot about that!" His father, a severe alcoholic, had taken him to the store and passed out drunk while trying to pay for their goods. The manager dragged his father to a nearby office. Jeff was left on his own, and he completed the check, including signing his father's name. He broke out in a nervous sweat, and his hands shook. Jeff had never done that before—what eight-year-old had? The shame reflected in the other shoppers' comments was burned into his very being. "I was always taking care of him, pretending he was sick. I was the parent. My mom left us and she told me I had to take care of my father."

Jeff reframed his experience in two sessions and practiced signing his name with the therapist until he could do it at work. Jeff also decided it was time to dig deeper into how his past—having parents who expected him to be a caretaker—had affected him.

Such powerful early training blends into an adulthood where it is automatic to worry about how others are faring and how they feel about you. It would be wonderful if this thinking magically ended at an appointed hour, and you'd be given a signal when you have taken care of others long enough. Then you could treat yourself as a real adult and put yourself first.

The impulse toward self-sacrifice fades the moment you choose to question if it is still necessary. The following questionnaire will help you assess where you might be sacrificing your own needs out of anxiety about the well-being and needs of others.

Self-Discovery Questionnaire: Are You Overly Responsible?

To help you uncover hidden beliefs or impulses, recall your reaction to a recent emotionally charged relationship problem, work stress, or family scene. Rank your identification with each statement using a scale of 0 to 5: 0 equals "Not me!" and 5 reveals a nearly perfect fit.

_____ *I get very anxious if anyone is late or doesn't show. I worry they're in trouble.*

_____ *I can't say no if someone wants my help, even if it takes hours out of my day.*

_____ *I am always apologizing. I include the receipt with a gift in case they don't like it.*

_____ *I feel uncomfortable having people see my home. I think they'll judge me.*

_____ *I often wake up feeling anxious. This can last all day, and I don't always know why.*

_____ *I worry about what other people are thinking about me. I review innocent interactions, and I search for how I might have been insensitive or stupid.*

_____ *I feel like a frightened child when anyone is angry with me, and I want to throw a tantrum.*

_____ *I'm a doormat. I always do more than my share. I smile, but secretly I feel resentful.*

_____ *I can't seem to find time for myself. I help and worry about others but have no time for exercise or rest.*

_____ *I believe that most people are better than I am. A master craftsman takes years to perfect his or her talent, and I think I should be terrific after a weekend class, so I don't continue.*

_____ *I admire others' efforts more than my own. I never measure up. I'm not sure why.*

_____ *I worry about being selfish. This stops me from scheduling time alone or for fun.*

_____ *I hate to ask for help or to bother people. I should be able to do everything myself.*

_____ *Compliments make me uncomfortable. I minimize my part, or I credit others when I am praised.*

Scoring: Add the numbers. The total measures your degree of unhealthy guilt and enmeshment, which clouds your ability to tend to your own needs.

0 to 10   You are remarkably calm and unaware of others' problems. It's possible you are a little too oblivious, maybe not doing your share. Compare your answers with those of a friend or family member.

11 to 25   Congratulations! You are aware of others but question the need and consequences before leaping to help.

26 to 40   Ask yourself how much you automatically do for others, and how much that costs you in terms of time for self-care.

41 to 65   You may want to seek help in lowering your sense of responsibility.

Low Self-Esteem Appearing as Self-Doubt

Healthy self-esteem celebrates the person you are becoming, as well as who you are right now. Low self-esteem reveals self-doubt. Some people who suffer from low self-esteem need to explain or apologize for every action, and others hide self-doubt with bravado and insults. Both types of people are dependent on praise because they don't know if they are doing well.

The next questionnaire will help you measure your view of yourself as a worthy person who has the right to feel confident about your own ideas. It offers some clues about to how to treat yourself with greater respect.

Self-Discovery Questionnaire: Self-Esteem vs. Approval from Others

Part 1. The following statements reflect how you feel about your current direction in life. Use a scale of 0 ("not me") to 5 ("me") to measure how much you identify with each one. You can break them down into smaller bites if necessary. For example, in the statement about important relationships, your life partner might get a 5, but your best friend who isn't so loyal these days would only rate a 2.

_____ *I embrace my daily habits and disciplines because they encourage my best self.*

_____ *I like how I look. I don't need to apologize if my car, house, or desk isn't neat.*

_____ *My most important relationships are loyal, healthy, and supportive.*

_____ *I feel confident that I am or will be successful in my chosen work.*

_____ *I like who I am and who I am becoming.*

_____ *I feel in charge of the current direction of my life.*

_____ *I consciously work on specific areas of self-improvement with a positive attitude.*

_____ *When I ask myself, "What do I want?" I am open to all feelings and sure of my answer.*

Part 2. These statements reflect how much you rely on others' approval versus your own. Use a scale of 0 ("not me") to 5 ("me") to measure how much you identify with each one. Acknowledge any progress you have made over the past few years.

_____ *I depend on others' opinions and hate to make big decisions without lots of help.*

_____ *I quiet negative self-talk by overusing alcohol, junk food, TV, or computer games.*

_____ *I look for quick fixes to big problems by looking in magazines or asking the advice of casual acquaintances.*

_____ *I do what professionals, family, or friends advise, even if it doesn't feel right to me.*

_____ *I copy the food choices, habits, and lifestyle of a new lover or new friend, even if I didn't like these things before. My schedule becomes whatever my friend's or lover's schedule is.*

_____ *I sometimes feel ashamed of my physical appearance.*

_____ *People would reject me if they knew who I really am and how worthless I feel.*

_____ *I deny or don't know my feelings and opinions much of the time.*

Scoring: Add the numbers from the first part, and then subtract the total from the second part. High numbers show more self-reliance. Instead of using the numbers to berate yourself, complete the questionnaire again when you finish this book and six months later. The questions should encourage you to build your self-trust and not criticize your life choices.

Self-Destructive Habits

We all seek comfort from the stress and hurts of life. Being good to yourself means treating yourself kindly, comforting yourself in ways that show self-love and self-esteem. Healthy comforts and rewards promote self-confidence and self-trust.

Your life isn't working when emotional pain and stress seem constant. The Adult thought is to seek self-improvement. Unfortunately, the idea of making necessary changes can feel overwhelming to the Child. Fear and frustration bring out the Protector, who wants to stop your pain. The Child and Protector don't have the capacity for long-range planning. The Adult is outvoted and succumbs to feeling that the anguish may never diminish and that next week is a better time to work on a plan.

Social habits such as smoking and overeating bring shame because others can witness this self-abusive cycle. Staying in abusive relationships reveals that we are weak, and shame is added to the feelings of being unworthy.

Hidden addictions are even more destructive to self-confidence. Drinking heavily, sexually dangerous liaisons, and overuse of medications may start out as self-comfort but lead to greater pain.

We know this and yet may continue to betray ourselves. The Protector has taken control and seems bent on self-destruction. It will resist change unless there is enough support for the Child. The Adult can give that support, especially with help from others. Acknowledging the shame and fear makes it possible for your Adult to take the small steps that lead to positive changes.

For Those Who Feel Stuck in Self-Betrayal

Many forms of addiction and compulsion can't be overcome by you alone. You are not weak, nor are you as alone as you feel. If you feel unable to escape the torment of self-betrayal, turn to a trusted friend or seek support from a professional.

Ask yourself if you are ready to leave the shame behind. Then call someone you believe you can trust and ask this person to support you. The beginning is that simple.

Ending the Cycle of Self-Betrayal

Whatever your personal issues, you are not as trapped as you may feel. Other people have overcome the forms of self-betrayal discussed in this chapter, have moved past their self-hate and fear, and have learned to trust themselves again. Most have developed deep faith along the way and found the joy of healthy relationships.

This book is here to support you on your journey toward self-love and confidence. Seek out the people and resources you need for guidance to continue on this path. Although you needn't go it alone, it's your job to *plan* what you want to achieve and how to get where you want to go. You can do this by considering what you are ready to change and what you want to achieve. There is great power in writing down your desired goals, even if you can't act on them instantly.

Consider what you think you are ready to change and what you want to achieve. There is great power in acknowledging a desire to change without the need to do it instantly. In chapter 10, there will be more tools to encourage self-trust.

This next exercise will warm up your mental engines and let your Child and Protector hear about any changes your Adult wants to embrace.

Self-Discovery Exercise: What Have You Already Changed? What Is Next?

This exercise encourages you to learn from your successes. It takes about thirty minutes and will give you a taste of setting positive goals without demanding that you achieve them immediately. Thinking about the challenges you've faced and the results you've achieved will remind you of how powerful you really are.

In your journal:

Step 1. Write down a list of positive changes you've made where you overcame a fear of failure or hardship. Examples: Quitting an unhealthy habit, completing training or college, moving somewhere alone, ending an enmeshed relationship, or working for a promotion.

Step 2. Choose one of these changes and note the details of your victory. Include fears, challenges, who supported you, and the results. Pay attention to what seemed like divine intervention and the lessons you learned. It doesn't need to be long, as you can see from the following example. Celebrate your ability to succeed.

Example: *I quit smoking pot after ten years of daily use. I had tried to quit or slow down many times before, but always fell back into it. Then I got pneumonia, and I had to quit when I was in the hospital. I saw a hypnotherapist twice after I was discharged, which helped. I called friends who had quit drinking through AA. They told me their stories and gave advice that helped me a lot. One result is I am healthy, but the best part is feeling free of compulsion and self-hate. I see I can ask for support from other people to face scary challenges.*

Step 3. Let the Adult, self-loving part of you write down a small positive change that you want to make. Write down the fears and resistance that the Child and Protector bring up. Note what you have done so far to try make this change, what could be the next step, and the results you hope to attain.

Example: *I really want to meditate for twenty minutes a day. My Child says I can't sit still that long. My Protector points out that I don't exercise or write in my journal enough already and that meditating is just one more thing that I'll fail to do. The truth is I do sit quietly a couple times for a few minutes during the week, but it's not enough to feel more peaceful, which is the result I want. I have a couple of meditation CDs I could put in the stereo and just listen to. It doesn't have to be in the morning. I may ask my roommate to join me. I could ask a friend who meditates if we could sit together the next time she visits. I know she'd like that.*

Repeat this exercise for as many issues as you like. Thinking about what you should do can feed self-hate, but putting it on paper acts as encouragement. Add to steps 1 and 2 as you think of old demons you've conquered and to step 3 with new ideas you'd like to explore. The purpose of this exercise is to open your heart to possibilities without expectation. In this way, you'll begin to become more the person you'd like to become and avoid the backlash of seeking comfort in unhealthy ways.

Refusing to betray yourself is as simple as holding tight to what is true and letting go of anything and anyone who discourages your efforts to succeed.

Preparing for the Next Chapter

Self-trust, faith in a positive future, and trusting others are the building blocks of the pattern of trust you use in making decisions about your life. This next chapter will help you see how well your pattern is working for you, and what you may want to change.

CHAPTER 7

Finding Your Trust Pattern

Can I free myself from the limits of my past?

It's natural to be thrown off balance when you think you're being betrayed or rejected. Your unique pattern of trust dictates how your mind and body initially react to such situations. This pattern is composed of the thoughts, feelings, and behavior uncontrolled by your thinking, Adult, self.

Your original pattern was produced in childhood, but your past doesn't have ultimate control over how you respond to conflict and betrayal in the present. If your current pattern of trust is working for you, that's great. If not, this chapter will help you to design and practice new ways to respond when trust feels uncertain.

What Is a Healthy Pattern of Trust?

A healthy pattern of trust results from a decision to strengthen trust in yourself and others while confirming your faith in a positive future. A healthy pattern of trust allows you to do the following:

- Acknowledge the emotions and physical reactions of the Child and Protector.

- Consider possible stories that reduce the likelihood of betrayal.

- Notice all thoughts that arise without judging or acting on them.

- Create thoughtful responses designed to reach a desired goal.

- Take action to resolve problems, relying on the compassion and wisdom of your Adult.

- Be open to a positive outcome.

Uncomfortable feelings that come from the Child and Protector shouldn't be ignored, nor should they be automatically acted upon. Problems arise when you attempt to deny or act on one of your feelings to the exclusion of the others, or when you become stuck in one element of a story.

A healthy pattern of trust requires you to acknowledge all of your thoughts and feelings as they arise. You also need to deliberately ask yourself questions to put the Adult back in charge. There is no magical order to the questions. What is important is that you keep the questions coming, helping to bring hidden feelings and beliefs to the surface.

The two trust foundation skills, The Trust Check-In (see chapter 2) and Finding Out What You Want (see chapter 4) use the responses from your Child and Protector to acknowledge your pain and move toward resolution. The following exercise will introduce you to a healthy pattern of trust and help you explore how your own pattern of trust operates.

_____

Self-Discovery Exercise: What Is Your Current Pattern of Trust?

As you read through the following story, put yourself into the father's position. Notice how his thoughts move from an involuntary loss of self-confidence to a conscious choice to think about how to create a positive future. This exemplifies a healthy pattern of trust.

John is a single father who arranged for his only son, Jesse, to have a credit card for emergencies and necessary expenses while at college. It had a low credit line, which the company raised without consulting John. Jesse knew about it. John opened the bill after spring break and sat down hard. Jesse had charged a thousand dollars for a skiing vacation. Jesse missed their regular Saturday morning telephone call, and John thinks he knows why.

Here is the series of feelings and thoughts that John had. You can recognize all the elements of a healthy pattern of trust:

Self-doubt: "I was wrong to trust him. How could I have been so stupid?"

Sadness, hurt: "I've been mother and father to Jim. How could he do this to me? To us?"

Anger, criticism: "He's an ingrate and a coward. He didn't even call."

Personalization: "Maybe he doesn't love me or respect me any more. I'm a fool."

Uncertainty about the future: "I can't act like this didn't happen. What do I do now?"

Resentment: "If that is all I mean, then no more credit card. He gets a job."

Concern for the other: "I bet he's plenty scared about this. He's afraid to call me."

Minimizing: "Maybe I've blown it out of proportion, but I'm not talking until he apologizes."

Choosing to trust: "He made a mistake, but it'll be a good lesson. I'm his dad and I'll call him."

In your journal:

To further explore your current pattern of trust, think of a time when you overreacted to a felt betrayal. Using John's pattern as a template, write down the thoughts and feelings that came up for you then. Notice the stages where you tended to get stuck and which stages you avoided. Owning up to the petty and irrational reactions that flicker through your mind will free you from them more quickly than denying or minimizing them.

Once you name your automatic reactions, you can then invite hidden feelings and thoughts by expressing the entire range of emotions. To do this, review your first set of responses and fill in any places you initially left blank with a few words.

The Three Types of Trust

The three types of trust—self-trust, faith in a positive future, and trust in others—form the foundation of your pattern of trust.

All three types are operating all the time, whether you are aware of them or not. As an example, if your trust in another is broken by a betrayal, you can feel self-confident that you'll manage to handle your flood of emotions. At the same time that you are feeling anxious about events that are immediately ahead, you can have faith that good will come from this for both of you.

A weakness in any of the three types of trust determines where you tend get stuck. If you are not very trusting of yourself or have little faith in a positive outcome, you may experience excessive doubt or fear. A lack of trust in others can result in the need to assign blame or the fear that they will blame you.

Thoughts and stories float through our minds without our asking. Many of us believe our responses are inferior to other people's. We keep our patterns of trust secret in an effort to appear normal and be accepted.

"I've Been Fooling Everyone"

Joan was invited by her pastor to study for the lay ministry. The pastor was surprised when she left a brief note saying she couldn't accept. He called her twice before she would agree to meet. The conversation began by Joan bursting into tears. "I don't deserve it," she explained. "I'm not good enough. I have terrible thoughts about other parishioners. I'm angry sometimes. I've fooled you into thinking I was a good person. God can't love me, and no one should."

Her pastor responded with compassion. "I have those same thoughts. Don't you know that everyone has unkind thoughts? It's because you work so hard to overcome them that I want you to help me serve the congregation. All I could ever ask of you is to keep working toward being a good person. You do that more than anyone I know."

Joan's critical and demanding parents had formed Joan's perception of herself, and she'd lived in terror that someone would find out about her terrible flaws. After talking with her pastor, she realized she'd been afraid for no reason. Joan accepted her pastor's invitation to study. She learned that she didn't have to accept any beliefs from her past if they didn't encourage her to be as loving and forgiving of herself as she tried to be with others.

In the above story, Joan appeared to everyone to be a caring and responsible person with great faith, but the conversation with her pastor revealed how weaknesses within the three types of trust undermined her ability to have a healthy pattern of trust. Her self-trust was focused on keeping quiet and protecting herself from being discovered to be hopelessly flawed. Although she longed for real faith in a benevolent God and a positive future, she didn't think she was worthy of blessings, no matter how hard she worked. She couldn't trust others with revealing her authentic self, since she was certain they would reject her if they really knew her.

Joan's pattern is not that unusual. Many people guess at what "normal" should be. They believe they don't have a cupful of the self-confidence that other people swim in. A fear of being rejected weakens the foundation of a healthy pattern of trust.

If you're like Joan, you may be afraid to reveal your true responses to life. Many of us contort our self-images to accommodate this irrational fear. This makes trust and intimacy a distant dream.

Improving Your Pattern of Trust

By consciously reinforcing the three types of trust, you'll find you can build a more solid foundation for a healthy pattern of trust. This next exercise will help you assess where to focus time and energy in your quest to become more trusting.

Self-Discovery Exercise:
Where Do You Get Stuck?

How do you react when you think that trust has broken down between you and someone you care about? Everyday occurrences like being stood up or a broken promise cause confusion in our closest relationships. The goal of this exercise is to discover where in the three types of trust you may be weak. This process will take about thirty minutes, and you can do it in stages or all at one time.

In your journal:

Choose a recent felt betrayal or misunderstanding and write about it. Read through the steps and the following example before picking up your pen.

Step 1. Recall the event and how you felt when you were trying to understand it without knowing the other side of the story. Write a brief summary of what happened, including the thoughts and feelings that came up for you.

Step 2. Can you see where you became stuck in the story? Where in your pattern of trust did you keep returning? To anger? Self-doubt? Confusion? Panic? How closely did your imagination and emotional responses match what you later learned was actually happening?

Step 3. Look at what you've written so far. What stands out in terms of your trusting of yourself, others, and the future outcome? Where may you have lost your Adult's perspective?

Step 4. What light does this shed on an older, deeper trust issue that still affects your current pattern of trust? What early experiences taught you to feel and believe the way you do? Who in your past are you reminded of?

Example:

1. I forgot a lunch date with an old friend and we set another time after my abject apology, "my treat." I confidently walked in five minutes early, and the hostess handed me this note: "I waited twenty minutes. I can't believe you did this again!" I felt devastated that I had gotten it wrong again and left my friend a telephone message expressing my stupidity and shame.

2. I believed she could never forgive me, that our ten-year friendship was lost. It took fifteen minutes to recognize I was overreacting. I sat quietly and asked, "What am I telling myself that is making me upset?" I saw how I feared she couldn't understand or forgive me. From a place of invoked faith, it occurred to me to review our e-mails and I saw she was the one who got the time wrong. I felt no anger at her. I was just giddy that I was off the hook. She called later with her *apology. We laughed about it and called each other the day of our next date to be sure we got it right.*

3. What I noticed about my strengths and weaknesses in the three types of trust was

- *I am quick to believe I am in the wrong. It's where I tend to feel stuck, "on the hook."*

- *I didn't trust her at first to understand and forgive me for a small mistake.*

- *It took me several minutes before I recalled there was a bigger view. I returned to my Adult by choosing to feel faith, and I remembered how important we are to each other.*

4. I see how forgiving I am of others' mistakes, but I don't trust they will forgive mine, or can recover from feeling betrayed as well as I do. I'd rather be wronged than be wrong. Being wrong in my family ended with ridicule. Mistakes were brought up years later, as "teasing," and were always hanging over my head. In writing this, it occurred to me that my mother always felt too guilty. I must have tried to be "good" like my mom, so I worry about others' feelings rather than my own.

The experience of splitting into younger selves tells us we need to pay attention to the choices we make. You will return to a sense of wholeness by reviewing what stories you tell yourself. The reward is the expansion of your ability to love and trust.

Some people face more of a challenge. Trust patterns that teeter on an absence of self-confidence and endless negativity require a thoughtful reexamination.

Unhealthy Trust Patterns

An unhealthy pattern of trust can lead you into stressful, sometimes dangerous relationships. You outwardly complain about the other person or situation but remain enmeshed. This focus on others allows you to deny your own problems and creates a self-defeating cycle that fosters distrust in yourself and almost everyone else.

Is Your Pattern of Trust Unhealthy?

Do you sometimes feel stuck in unhealthy patterns? Review the list below and note if you tend to fit into one of the patterns. Delight in any that you have permanently escaped.

- If your boss, partner, best friends, and children seem to take advantage of you, your distrust of others may be unconscious. You may be afraid to ask them for what you want out of fear that they will criticize you.

- If you stay in jobs, relationships, residences, or friendships that aren't satisfying, you may lack trust in your own abilities and judgment.

- A lack of faith in a positive future can keep you from reaching for bigger dreams and healthier choices in comforts, work, and relationships.

Unhealthy patterns are often caused by a history of loss or cruelty. Those who didn't experience a tragedy can also feel adrift, not knowing who and how much to trust. Children who were overprotected may become adults who feel incapable of taking risks. They hang onto hopeless jobs, fear their own children's anger, and tolerate disrespect from peers. They feel they have no choice but to stay with the people in their lives.

Redesigning Your Pattern of Trust

Building trust challenges childhood fears. Over time, you can take increasingly bigger risks and find freedom and faith. The following story tells of someone who completely changed her pattern of trust.

She worked hard to reclaim self-trust and faith after years of trusting someone who failed her. She was able to build trust and intimacy in ways she never thought possible.

"I Learned to Trust Myself"

Josie was in her early fifties and had been married for thirty years. Her doctor referred her to a therapist after she suffered several panic attacks. "My husband, Don, and I moved to this small town two years ago to make a fresh start after he'd had an affair," she told her therapist. "We decided to build our home, and I moved up to supervise construction. He kept an apartment in the city near his work, promising to visit every weekend. By the end of the first year, he was using the demands of his job as an excuse to stay away all but one weekend a month. On one of his rare visits, I found recent e-mails on Don's computer from the woman he had promised to never see again. I confronted him, and he assured me it was over.

"He apologized, insisting he hadn't been unfaithful except for writing to her. He agreed to couples counseling, which I took as a sign he really wanted to work things out. The counselor supported the idea that he should look for work near our home and give up the apartment. He balked at the idea, and I began to have anxiety attacks. I feel totally trapped: I can't stand the idea of being on my own, but I can't trust him. I don't know what to do."

Josie initially described Don to her therapist as "a good person who made a mistake, whom I trust with my life. He's a talented artist, helpful, good company, and great with money. I married him when I was just twenty-two. My mother told me to get married and not try to live alone. 'The world is filled with hardship. Settle down and be safe,' she said. Don seemed nice enough, so I didn't date anyone else, and I felt safe having a husband. I was shy and training to be a teacher, which I didn't really want to do. I always wanted children and thought I wouldn't have to teach because I'd be a stay-at-home mom. Don told me the third year we were married that he didn't want the responsibility of children, and I went along because he threatened to leave if I got pregnant."

She begged Don to spend more time in their new home. Josie was afraid he'd return to the affair or begin a new one. She was stuck wanting him to love her, to be faithful, and to move closer, but she knew unconsciously that she shouldn't trust him. Her anxiety attacks were caused by her Adult self telling her she had to let him go, but that was too terrifying for her Child. "I can't take care of this big house alone, and he's the only family I have. I want to trust him. Why can't I? What is wrong with me?"

She saw how she had idealized Don as she looked deeper into their lives. He was marginally employed, had few friends, visited less and less, and demanded to have access to the money she had inherited.

Josie was stuck in enmeshment, with no self-trust or faith. She was forcing herself to trust someone who betrayed her. She began to realize how capable she had become since living apart. She also saw Don was selfish and incapable of managing his own life, let alone hers. Josie grew less angry with Don as she needed him less. She had lied to herself in order to keep the structure of a marriage, but her deeper intuition had told her he was holding her back from a wonderful life.

This brought her to the determination to build trust in herself before she decided about the marriage. Two years into therapy, she was employed at a job she loved, traveling on her own, taking fun classes, and making new friends.

The day she took off her wedding ring and called an attorney was both terrifying and liberating. "I know what I want now, and I know I can handle what life brings."

You can promote self-awareness and self-confidence by being honest about how you feel, whether with others or in your private journal. Begin by asking yourself, "How free am I to be myself and show my true feelings and opinions around other people?"

Self-Discovery Exercise:
How Deep Is Your Trust for Others?

This exercise will help you gain valuable information about your unconscious pattern of trust.

In your journal:

Draw two vertical lines, creating three columns. The first will hold names of people you know and the next two are for notes. Set aside at least twenty minutes. You can continue to add names as you wish.

Column 1. Begin the list with people you frequently see. You will *not* be sharing this list with anyone. Include anyone you need to interact with, such as coworkers, neighbors, family members, as well as those whom you seek out either by habit or intentionally.

Column 2. Using pure intuition, give a rating of 0 to 100 to note how relaxed and confident you feel with each person. This measures your trust with key people in your life. Be curious and don't judge the first number that comes to mind. You are not indicting anyone as untrustworthy, and you can change the number as you go along. You are simply noting how free or cautious you feel with this person about revealing who you really are. This can include sharing creative ideas, big dreams, and politics. Every relationship has areas of discomfort or dissimilarity. Feeling comfortable with these limits doesn't lower the number.

Note: If doing this exercise makes you tense, take a breath, and ask yourself, "What rule am I breaking here?" Ask with the next breath, "*Whose* rule am I breaking?" Now is a good time to add to the first column, your parents, teachers, and ex-lovers who may no longer be in your life. How free did you feel to be authentic around them? Keep adding names to the first column and numbers to the second column without worrying about the outcome, and let your Child and Protector participate in the voting.

Expand this list as you become more skilled. Are there customers, clients, or employees with whom you feel especially comfortable or guarded?

Column 3. Look over the list of people and the ratings. Write down any qualities about each person that caused you to feel safer or more apprehensive. Are they younger, less experienced, or nonconfrontational? Are people who are self-confident easier or harder for you to trust? Do you feel you have to play a role with someone, being the "big sister," being funny, or playing down how smart you are? To be encouraged to be your best is terrific. Acting as if you are something you don't feel you are cuts into intimacy and mutual trust.

Old stories have controlled your trust pattern. Now you can design your own by focusing on the positive stories that say you deserve respect and that others can be trusted.

Pay attention to how you react each time you are out of balance. Ask yourself what would make you happier and more resilient. This will help identify the stories and feelings that lead to self-trust and a deeper faith in a positive future.

Preparing for the Next Chapter

Real trust in others is validated by long experience and serves to help us grow and expand our courage. Choosing to give and receive trust is an act of wisdom and emotional resilience. In the next chapter, you will be preparing to take the risk of revealing your authentic self.

Review the exercises you've done in this chapter. This will guide you in taking the steps that lead to sharing your truth with those you want to trust even more.

CHAPTER 8

Building Trust
with Others

How can I develop more understanding and compassion?

When you trust others, you no longer want to control them. You want to understand and support them and are able to ask for their understanding and support in return. You increase your capacity to listen to hard truths when you know you can survive, even thrive, if a relationship doesn't turn out as you'd hoped. You can dare to be honest about who you are, and what you feel. Faith helps you open your heart even wider. It takes great effort to heal past hurts. Feeling safe to trust others is your reward.

In chapter 4, you looked at past betrayals and how you could have handled them with greater skill. In this chapter, you will choose where you want to feel more belonging and intimacy. You'll learn to prepare for and invite others into conversations that increase understanding and intimacy.

You may wonder if it's worth revealing your authentic self for the chance of greater trust and intimacy. Here are the results that make the risk worthwhile:

- Assumptions are cleared without the agony of mind reading and delay.

- Genuine apologies are exchanged without shame and punishment.

- Broken rules are addressed without rancor.

- Misunderstandings no longer cause that old panic that the relationship is over.

Building Trust with Understanding

Mutual understanding begins to grow the moment you choose to hear another's truth and share yours. You no longer worry about what should have been said and what someone should feel.

Every time you reveal your authentic self, you take a risk. However, you must do this to produce more understanding and connection. Still, the idea of exploring a conflict may make you nervous. Building more trust means releasing the tight grip that the Child and Protector have on your ability to risk rejection.

Making It Safe to Talk Things Over

The tools in this chapter will put your Adult safely in charge. You'll learn what you want to give and receive as you improve communication with someone else and increase mutual trust.

Using the communication tools and techniques in this chapter may feel awkward at first. Unfortunately, very few of us witnessed a natural model of communication using compassion and fairness as guides. I encourage you to swallow any embarrassment and admit to your friend, coworker, or partner that you feel safer using these tools to ensure fairness.

These strategies will help a worthwhile relationship move deeper into your circles of belonging. You might discover the relationship isn't as durable as you'd hoped. This is just one of the fears that often keeps us from exploring conflicts in our relationships. The benefits of these explorations will far outweigh the costs, both now and in the future. This chapter helps you to face your fears head on.

Preparing for More Understanding

We all link giving bad news with hurting others and the possibility of rejection. The fear of making someone upset can cause anyone to regress in age. The Child appears and is terrified, followed by the Protector, who will numb us or make us afraid to speak.

The Child's fears will arise when you want to risk being more intimate or ask for a commitment. You wouldn't dream of making a speech without preparing beforehand. Preparation is just as important when working on a challenging issue with someone you care about. Let's start with choosing the right time.

The Importance of Timing

Timing isn't everything, but it is important. Have you ever waited until the anxiety was so great that you couldn't speak without bursting into tears or exploding in anger? You may have mentally rehearsed for days, then blurted out your whole message as he or she got into the car. What you wanted to say with dignity sounds overwrought and confusing, even to you.

Abrupt and intense scenes scare many people off from trying to resolve conflicts. Carefully prepare before talking about important issues. Methodical timing and a deliberate pace make hard conversations run smoother.

Preparing on Your Own

Practice on a small issue with someone with whom you feel quite safe. If there is a pressing issue and you feel ready, begin there. You're learning a new skill, so be patient with yourself.

The following three tools can help you prepare for an important conversation. These tools can increase your compassion and confidence. As you read about and try out each tool, imagine you are addressing the same person and issue.

First Preparation Tool:
Five Steps toward Honesty

These five steps will help you speak with honesty and compassion. They calm the Child's fears and are best done in the following order:

1. Explore thoughts and feelings privately by writing down the reactions of the Child, Protector, and Adult.

2. Address past sources of strong feelings: childhood or a first-time experience.

3. Ask your Adult to assess the real and current danger or limits of the situation.

4. Identify and toss aside false assumptions.

5. If the risk seems worthwhile, break the ice by inviting a conversation.

You can use this tool to explore how you hide your true self from people you care about. The goal is to increase trust and understanding with people you like and with whom you want to feel closer.

In your journal:

Choose a person with whom you would like more intimacy or to explore a small conflict. Select something you haven't revealed that would help this person know you better. Your likes and dislikes, pet peeves, dreams, and phobias are unique. If you think it could increase intimacy and trust if he or she shared something similar, you have a good topic. Write down the person, subject, and your fear about possible reactions in a sentence. Use the following questions (an expansion on the five steps above) to guide your thoughts. Write your responses as you consider each one. Read the example before you start.

1. On a scale of 1 (minor) to 10 (major), how much does your Child fear rejection or ridicule?

2. What story do you tell yourself that stops you from being honest?

3. Where might you have learned this? Name the specific incidents.

4. What's your Adult's worst-case scenario?

5. Could you handle that result? If no, choose another issue. Wait for "Yes, I can live with it."

6. Has the number on your fear of rejection scale changed? What is it?

7. If you feel comfortable, arrange a time to meet, so you can tell the other person that you want to share something.

Example:

Megan is a forty-five-year-old single woman who is a full-time teacher. She has secretly dreamed of studying art in Paris. "I've saved the money to attend art school for a year, but I've not told my best friend, Lucy, who also teaches with me. I'm afraid she'll feel abandoned and be devastated. My fear of rejection is 8. Lucy's husband left her a year ago, and we visit or call almost every evening. I'm afraid of hurting her or making her mad. Where did I learn this? I moved back with my lonely, widowed mother after college, rather than go out on my own. Someone else's pain always feels more important then my needs. Realistic scenario? Lucy is a terrific friend and we'd e-mail, or she could even visit! She'd probably be more hurt if I didn't trust her to tell her my dream because I thought she'd deny me this joy. My fear is now about a 3 and falling fast. I'll ask her to talk tomorrow night, telling her I have a dream I want to share."

You can expand your skills later by using this tool on other relationships, or different issues with the same person. By doing this a few times on paper, you'll learn to quickly go through the process mentally. For now, move on to the next tool, using the same person and issue you just addressed. If you choose someone else, go back to the first tool, and ask yourself the same questions.

Second Preparation Tool:
The Yin-Yang of Understanding

We often waste time anticipating what someone else will say, ready to counter it with some brilliant counter argument. Speaking the truth and inviting others to say theirs is far more efficient. This second preparation tool focuses on the trust you want others to experience during an important exchange. Your commitment to trust will promote mutual understanding. The hurts that prolong distrust will fade after you both feel understood.

In your journal:

Draw a circle about six inches in diameter, and divide it in half using a yin-yang curve.

Step 1. On one side of the circle, write: "What do I want to (a) hear, (b) see, and (c) feel while sharing my truth?" Then sit quietly and consider your answers. Imagine seeing the person's face and hearing his or her words and tone of voice. What facial expression are you hoping for? What physical sensations (relaxed, awake, tender, protected) do *you* want to feel? Write your responses.

Step 2. On the opposite side, write: "What do I want this person to (a) hear, (b) see, and (c) feel during our exchange?" Close your eyes and imagine him or her looking at you while listening to your voice. How do you wish this person to feel in his or her body? Write down what you saw and felt.

Step 3. Review what you've written with tender concern for your Child. Is it safer for your younger self, who was afraid to bring it up before? Does your Protector tell you that it can't be this easy, it's a trick? Calm their fears with kindness and honesty.

You'll be amazed at how prepared you become using these two tools.

The third preparation tool polishes your presentation with a rehearsal. You will invoke faith to help you remember that everything turns out for the best.

Third Preparation Tool:
Having Faith in a Positive Outcome

Close your eyes and keep your journal nearby. Visualize a time in the near future when the actual conversation could take place. Imagine what it would be like to stand in the background, calmly watching your prepared self and the other person you want to reconnect with. See yourselves together like characters in a play. Focus compassionate attention on the other person. Notice how he or she appears to be feeling and send positive thoughts and loving energy in his or her direction.

Focus in the same way on your future self. Notice how nervous, vulnerable, or close to tears your future self may be. Now step into the body of the other person and feel his or her sensations. What do you feel toward your future self from this position? What makes you want to trust or distrust? Slip out of the other person and take a breath, then slip into your future self again. What makes you want to have this conversation? Is there anything else you need to know before you enter the actual event?

In your journal:

Write down any insights about how to increase the feelings of safety and compassion between you. If, at the end of these exercises, you still don't feel comfortable enough to invite contact, choose another person and run through the three preparation tools. You'll find that you'll eventually be able to use these tools effortlessly and without writing. However, writing down your responses in the beginning is the ticket to success.

Facing Your Fear of Rejection

The greatest barrier to approaching someone else is the fear of rejection. Many people stop themselves from talking by assuming it will make the problem worse. They don't know how to begin.

Alexandra Sascha Wagner found her poet's voice through the grief of losing her two children. Her poem touches deep into what matters most. She expresses the reason to face your fears of reaching out and being willing listen.

Did you know?
When we truly listen
to each other,
we are saying
—I love you—
(Wagner 1999)

The desire for deep connection is a natural instinct. This instinct was dimmed as we learned that if we did not agree, speaking up could bring rejection or punishment. Guessing what others were feeling was much safer, even when we were wrong. Making assumptions and hiding uncomfortable truths became habits.

These habits were intended to save us from rejection. We may not realize they are habits until we really want to know what someone else is thinking and feeling. Asking a straightforward question will feel awkward after years of practicing subterfuge. We are now faced with believing real answers and releasing the stories of unworthiness we've created.

Making Assumptions Causes Rejection

The Child wants to believe that when people say they love each other, they understand everything that each other wants, without the awkward process of revealing their secret stories. When a truth slips out and doesn't match the Child's assumptions, it feels like another betrayal because the truth challenges the certainty that existed moments before.

Don Miguel Ruiz expands on this idea, saying the biggest assumption that humans make is to believe "that everyone sees life the way *we* do. . . . And this is why we have a fear of being ourselves around others. Because we think everyone else will judge, victimize, abuse, and blame us as we do ourselves. So even before others have a chance to reject us, we have already rejected ourselves" (1997, 69).

By admitting that you can't know what other people feel or want, you can break the assumption habit. Use the second foundation skill, Finding Out What You Want, (see chapter 4) with yourself, and then stretch your trust by sharing what you are thinking and what you want. The bravest step is inviting the other person to talk. Comparing each other's stories may seem frightening at first, but it stops the assumptions that underlie old fears of rejection.

Breaking the Ice

Not knowing what is going to happen or what someone is thinking about you can create a tension and coldness between two people. Breathing becomes difficult, and yet you can't quite say what is really the matter.

Stephen Covey describes understanding as the oxygen in the room of relationships (1988). Two people may want to talk things out, but they see each other holding back tears and rage. They're both drowning in resentments born of assumptions. They feel safer being right and have given up being loved. Worse yet, they are afraid to be vulnerable. They need to break the ice.

How to Begin and What to Avoid

It's scary to begin difficult conversations. Knowing how will give a great boost to your confidence. It's just as important to avoid the overtures that sabotage the best intentions. *Do not* use the following phrases as your initial strategy. Imagine someone leaving them as messages on your answering machine and you'll understand why. (You can imagine the voice tinged with irritation.)

These phrases come from the Protector. They terrify the Child self, which unleashes the Protector, who is ready to do battle.

- "We need to talk."

- "We've got a problem."

- "How many times do I have to ask . . . ?"

- "Why haven't you . . . ?"

These next phrases come from the self-absorbed Child. They will create denial and irritation before you can hear the actual issues.

- "I know you are angry with me" or "I don't know why you are angry with me."

- "You don't love me anymore. If you did, you wouldn't have ..."

- "Promise you won't get mad."

- "I know you're thinking ... , but you have no right to think that way."

Do the phrases above reflect how you and a partner or associates tend to lead off discussions? Conversations that begin with these phrases quickly become fights and produce no understanding. They are barely disguised efforts to control another's feelings and to avoid taking responsibility.

Respectful and Honest Invitations to Talk

The goal is to express yourself from the heart. If you are initially rebuffed, ask if you can contact them later. Imagine inviting someone to talk over a mutual concern. You want each of you to feel safe and ready to listen. Practice saying the following and imagine hearing them, and notice your Child's response:

- "We've had a misunderstanding, and I'd like to work to make it better."

- "I miss you and our trusting each other."

- "I really want to talk, but I'm feeling scared to make it worse. How about you?"

- "Our relationship is important to me. What do you think we can do?"

- "I'm feeling sad that we've lost our trust."

- "It's been a while, and I don't want to let our relationship slip away. What can I do to make you feel safe talking with me?"

- "I sense something isn't sitting well with you. Is it about us? If so, I'd like to hear it."

- "I've been thinking about what happened. I want to listen to what you have to say."

These phrases have a deliberate softness, and they reveal vulnerability and the desire to connect. They invite the other to help set the tone and a time for your conversation.

A More Direct Approach

Sometimes you need to take a deep breath and dive into the issue. This approach works best when you believe the other person will trust your concern and appreciate your candor. This next group of phrases is more immediate and direct.

- "I feel that we're in conflict about.... I'd like to resolve it, how about you?"

- "I have something important to say to you about.... Is now a good time for you to talk?"

- "Are you angry or upset?" and if the answer is yes, then say, "Are you angry or upset at me?"

Notice how your Child responds in the following story.

"Are You Angry at Me?"

Mary was a receptionist at a public health office. She looked up from her desk one afternoon to see a red-faced fireman in uniform storm into the office. He pounded his fist on the counter and shouted, "Where is that damn doctor? And don't try to protect him!"

Her first thought was to drop to the floor, but instead she stood, took a breath, and calmly asked, "Sir, are you angry?" "Yes!" came the answer. "Are you angry at me?" Flustered, the fireman spoke more quietly, "No, unless you are hiding that cowardly doctor who drove right past the bloody accident we were dealing with!" (He saw the county parking permit for a medical doctor on the car's bumper.) Mary explained that she'd been there for three hours, and no doctor had come in or was scheduled to come in. "I understand why you are angry," she said. "But please don't take it out on me. I think it might have been the mental health division doctor who drove by." She walked the fireman next door to the mental health office and asked the receptionist if the psychiatrist had come in, which he had. The fireman was grateful to Mary. His anger was acknowledged and he quickly calmed down.

Imagine having your teenager, spouse, or boss run up to you in a huff. Practice breathing and standing up bravely and asking, "Are you angry or upset?" Wait for the other person's answer and follow with "Are you angry or upset with me?" Express real curiosity in your tone. Make it clear you won't participate in the other person's frustration. You are leading the way to understanding by hearing the answers.

Facing Those You Have Wronged

It's hard to face people after you've broken trust or hurt them. Don't cause them more suffering by making them initiate the conversation. You'll bury any hopes for understanding or building trust under assumptions and stories. Keeping yourself and others in limbo will destroy trust more surely than admitting your guilt and remorse.

Get straight to the point. Use the "Five Steps toward Honesty" and "The Yin-Yang of Understanding" to prepare. Explain to your Child and Protector that you must acknowledge the problem, regardless of the outcome. Then try out one of these statements.

- "I'm feeling very guilty about something. I owe you the truth."

- "I behaved badly and didn't stop myself. You didn't deserve it, and I take full responsibility."

- "There is something that I am scared to tell you. I'm afraid you'll reject me, but I'd like you to listen all the way through. I'll listen to you whenever you feel like talking about it."

Relationships give us endless opportunities to hurt those we love, no matter how hard we try to avoid it. Being human guarantees this will happen. Do the work to prepare for a meeting. Break the ice and promise the other person you will listen to his or her assumptions and feelings without interruption or argument. Invite the other person to talk as quickly as you can.

Your compassion for the others' pain will invite them to share even more deeply. You'll both learn to listen to each other's Child and appreciate the Protector. This is intimacy at its best.

Preparing for the Next Chapter

You've tried many methods of comforting your Child and calming the Protector to allow you to be more honest in your relationships. Chapter 9 is focused on facing the challenge of relationships that are losing ground in trust and intimacy.

Consider any relationships that you feel are beyond your courage and skills. You may need to move them further out of your circles of belonging. People who are dangerous to you or your dependents are not candidates for trust, no matter how much you want to understand and love them.

The techniques found in this book will fall short of helping you recover a relationship subjected to repeated betrayals. For that, I recommend you seek mediation or counseling together. Some people you care for are simply not trustworthy. They have problems that you can't fix. The next chapter looks at deciding if you really want to salvage a damaged or seemingly hopeless relationship.

CHAPTER 9

The Hardest Decision: Go or Stay?

How can I know when to say good-bye?

It takes two people to create a relationship and only one to end it. If you're sacrificing your happiness to stay in any relationship, it's time to uncover what's stopping you from asking for more or deciding to leave. You have two logical, Adult-pleasing choices when a once vital relationship has become unhealthy or stale: rebuild the trust with honesty, or end your connection as kindly as possible. Unfortunately, many people choose to hang on for too long despite broken promises and general incompatibility.

This chapter explores reasons why you may hang on to painful relationships, and how to build the self-trust you'll need if you decide it's time to go.

Why Is Leaving So Hard?

Staying in a self-destructive situation keeps us lost in shame and self-doubt. Every day we awaken to the pain and ask ourselves, "Why don't I leave?" Do any of these situations sound familiar?

- staying in a stressful job where you try to please a critical supervisor or are afraid to desert your coworkers

- conducting a love affair with someone who is married or refuses to make a commitment

- being in one-sided relationships with dependent people

- having friends who demand lots of your attention, resenting you if you say no

- defending the qualities of a lover your friends dislike, despite your own unhappiness

- keeping abuse secret, believing your partner won't do it again, and that it's proof he or she needs more love

- hoping that a self-absorbed parent will someday respect you

The following exercise will help you reflect upon past or current experiences where you felt or feel unable to leave an unhappy situation. Exploring these memories may be painful, but it can help you address unmet needs and change any beliefs that caused you to feel trapped.

Self-Discovery Exercise: Do You Stay Too Long?

Allow plenty of time to remember details of situations and feelings about when you have stayed too long in situations or relationships. Writing down the important insights takes about thirty minutes.

In your journal:

Step 1. Write a sentence or two about past experiences where you felt stuck. (Hint: To jog your memory, you can use the list of situations described above.) Are you still emotionally torn?

Step 2. Reflect on current situations where you wonder if you should leave. Feel the hopes and fears that keep you from leaving.

Do you trust your intuition to tell you if a situation is right for you? Do you trust your intuition when it says something is wrong? Write a sentence that captures the details of what's happening and feelings that come up.

Step 3. Write down both the illogical and the practical reasons for staying in relationships where you felt stuck. Financial dependency, religious authority, and deep commitments can figure into this. Ask your Child and Protector to voice their concerns. Is your Adult telling you what you can do?

You can learn to listen to your Child with Adult compassion. Accept that your younger self may hang on to the slimmest of hopes that the situation will improve. It is the job of your Adult to nurture and protect your Child. This includes making a firm decision that you have given the situation a fair chance.

When Can You Say You've Tried Enough?

No one benefits by clinging to a relationship when the trust is gone. However, shared connections and occasional good times can hold us hostage in uncertainty. When leaving is the obvious choice, it still feels daunting to face the expected upheaval. It's natural to wonder if it's the right thing to do.

Most of us have tried "one more time" to salvage a hopeless relationship, long after recognizing how self-destructive it has become. Still, we eventually were able to break the spell or survive the rejection. These questions can linger after we've healed: "Why didn't I walk away when I felt it was horrendous? What made me so afraid?"

Mira Kirshenbaum explains part of the dilemma in her book *Too Good to Leave, Too Bad to Stay*. The choice to take care of ourselves by leaving is countered by thinking, "I'd better not make a decision until I see what's best for everyone" (1996, 13). Both parties seldom see leaving as the "best choice." Whoever starts the discussion will feel anxious and guilty, and the other will feel hurt and rejected. We delay the ending because the shock of separation is more frightening that the dull ache of disappointment.

When You Know It Is Over, But You Still Can't Go

There comes a time when you know it's over. Your unhappiness about the relationship is a constant theme in your life. You've convinced everyone you're miserable and need to leave. Friends, family, and your therapist support your decision, yet cutting the connection remains impossible. Why is this so difficult?

Three cords bind us to difficult relationships: *enmeshment, ambivalence,* and *fear of abandonment.* Each is a form of emotional dependency. We rely on others for our sense of well-being and become unable to act on our own behalf. We believe we're better off in the relationship, no matter how bad.

- Enmeshment is created by basing your self-esteem on other people's approval and affirmation. When you stay in a relationship mainly to please or take care of the other person, you've traded self-respect for being needed.

- Ambivalence erodes confidence in the logical Adult self. Self-trust is sacrificed in order to feel loved, which makes being emotionally honest difficult.

- Fear of abandonment is lodged so deeply in the Child self, it feels like dying to say good-bye. There is a lack of faith, which creates a terror of ending up alone.

You're not limited to having just one of these three issues. Most of us have struggled with all of them. Explore your Child's fears as you look at the issues one at time. This will help your Adult self acknowledge the support you need to make the difficult changes that will release you from unhealthy situations. Although romantic partnerships often dominate the topic of "go or stay," the uncertainty about knowing the right thing to do can show up in any relationship.

Pay attention to your mind-body responses as you continue reading. Take note of how current friendships, work environments, and family patterns may reveal a tug-of-war within you. The tools and stories provided here are meant to help you decide to invest more energy trying to improve unsatisfying relationships.

The Secret Fear: You're Unworthy of Real Love

What could stop you from prevailing over old fears? The answer stems back to a fear of being secretly flawed. You believe you're not worthy to attract someone terrific, so you settle for what you have. What torments marvelous people into thinking they are unworthy of love? Consider this list of common childhood experiences:

- secret sexual or physical abuse of any size or duration

- ridicule by older siblings and bullies, disguised as "teasing"

- abandonment or the death of your primary source of care and love

- being told you were selfish if you had special needs, or conceited if you had talent

- being told you were ugly or being shunned for wearing glasses, braces, or hand-me-downs

- a visible difference that caused rejection, such as a different skin color or body size

- diagnosis with a learning disability or segregation to a "special" class

- comparisons to more scholarly siblings or being told you're underachieving

- taunts for early sexually development or being told you were sexually undesirable

- frequent moves, never connecting for long with peers or teachers

- your parent saying, "I wish I'd never had kids. I would leave this marriage if it weren't for you."

Self-Discovery Exercise:
What Still Makes You Feel Unworthy

No one escapes childhood without feeling loss and shame. Even the popular kids had secret hurts and doubts.

In your journal:

Recall and write down insults from others and the awful things you have believed about yourself. You might laugh about it now, but if you spent your adolescence obsessed about your thighs or about wearing glasses or braces, include them.

Step 1. For ideas, refer to the list at the beginning of this chapter. List the names, incidents, and feelings they evoke. Include a current boss or friend who bullies you. What hurtful things do your partner, siblings, and parents say to you? Do they bring up painful history as "funny" stories?

Step 2. Circle those memories that still sting. Do you still think you're too fat to find love, that you talk too fast, or you aren't very smart? Do you still feel you are "damaged goods" from childhood abuse or are unlovable because your dad left when you were young?

Step 3. Refer to the memories that still have power; convert what people said into more positive, self-caring language. These honest statements will help you stop betraying yourself. Each one may point to something you really want to address. Bring it up in therapy, or share your story with those that you trust to listen with compassion.

Examples:

- "I'm too fat to be loved" becomes the affirmation "I may be twenty pounds heavier than I want to be, but I love myself, and I am loved by many wonderful people."

- "No one could want me because I was raped" becomes the affirmation "My body is mine! I reclaim my sexuality and will share it only when it feels right for me."

- "I'm not as smart as my sister" becomes the affirmation "We are different. I choose to concentrate on my own talents and stop resenting and competing with my sister."

Powerful negative thoughts survive if you never challenge them. They linger as vague feelings of inadequacy. These scars can stop you from walking away from current abusive or inadequate relationships. The charge will fade when you convert them into affirmations and claim them as your own.

The Sticky Web of Enmeshment

It's difficult to leave people who have convinced you that they need you to live. Your intuition tells you it's time to move on when conflicts arise and they say hateful things. You feel a sense of freedom in a precious moment of clarity. The dependent ones can sense this. They express remorse and beg you to stay, and promise that "things will be better," but discussing your needs in the relationship threatens them.

When people are trapped in "learned helplessness" (Seligman 1998), they reject all suggestions of how to become more effective and independent. When pressed to seek help about the relationship, they insist they're happy with the way things are. Conditions that promote this are

- chronic depression

- anxiety and severe phobias

- hypochondria and physical ailments that are used as excuses

- low self-esteem and no self-trust

- chronic failure to keep jobs and friendships, never developing potential

- addictions that undermine function and capacity for self-care

- destructive personality disorders

People who can't cope with the responsibilities of their lives don't know what they feel beyond desperation, anger, and fear. They live in denial and refuse to seek help, and they are terrified of being left or controlled. They need someone to depend on but are afraid of genuine intimacy.

Escaping the Guilt of Enmeshment

Enmeshment is an unequal relationship. You become the parent of an adult who is afraid to grow up. The other person's problems and inadequacies stand in the way of your goals and dreams. He or she is helpless, and you are competent. The other person may threaten suicide when faced with criticism or rejection, or he or she may act out violently. How can you leave someone who is ill or on the edge of self-destruction? Unhealthy guilt makes leaving very difficult.

Self-Discovery Exercise: Do You Seek Out People Who Need You?

This is a brief screening of your past and present relationships. Include all situations. The intention is to honestly assess if you have (or had) a magnetic attraction to situations where you feel obligated to put your own needs and goals aside. It will take about fifteen minutes to do.

In your journal:

Step 1. Many of us have had a history of relationships with dependent people. We stayed too long with lovers who had a horrible childhood or addictions, or our childhood friends were the sickly or shy "odd ones." We heard, "I know I can depend on you!" more than most. Write down any relationships that come to mind, from elementary school to the present.

Step 2. Recall where you learned to do this and who your models were. Did you have parents who needed you to be the adult? Did you know more than you wanted to about your parents' finances and personal problems, including sex life? Were you expected to keep others' secrets and worried about other people being caught?

Step 3. Be honest and ask yourself if you still live this pattern. This includes volunteering more than you can afford, not charging full fees for your services, and trying to rescue family members and friends. Write down any relationship or situation where you feel enmeshed.

Step 4. Complete this sentence for each current enmeshed situation: "If I stopped _____ , I'm afraid that _____ will _____ ." Examples: "If I stopped doing the cooking and cleaning, I'm afraid that no one will do it." "If I quit my job, I'm afraid that my coworkers will be burdened and the clients will suffer."

You can have healthy and intimate relationships with people who have major challenges. People with physical, emotional, or financial struggles often have an independent spirit and do much of their own self-care. You are not enmeshed if there is mutual support and you both feel free to go or stay.

Sorting Out Ambivalence

Ambivalence is a tangle of two strong opposing emotions. You are torn by the intensity of going back and forth, as you feel the potency of each. Psychologist in the early twentieth century used the word "ambivalence" to help their patients identify the effects of having two mutually exclusive feelings at the same time: love and hate, fear and longing, and rage and lust. Relationship ambivalence is the result of problems that seem to improve but then reappear. You feel fabulous and confident about your communication one day, then anxious beyond tolerance the next. The foundation is shaky because one or both of you cannot make a real commitment to resolving conflicts or making positive changes.

A clear sense of yes or no about continuing the relationship is hidden by the fog of "maybe." If you don't make a decision as time moves on, you no longer trust your own feelings and stop asking for what you really want. You move between vague dissatisfaction and hoping things would be good again. Self-loathing and self-doubt replace the self-love and enthusiasm that marked the beginning of the relationship.

Fighting and making up are tolerated because they remind you of the early passion, and the truth spills out for a few hours. Later you realize that making any decision is better than passivity. That is the job for your Adult. To the Child, "positive change" is an oxymoron. "When in doubt, do nothing" might be the motto of the scared and helpless Child.

Challenging the Fear of Abandonment

Are you are staying in an unhappy situation because you emotionally collapse at the thought of separating? The thought of being alone raises fear of abandonment. You might also fear that you couldn't tolerate the pain of the early phase of separation. This can be embarrassing to admit. As adults, we think we should be beyond the irrational need of having someone to be with. The following story illustrates how powerful this need can be.

"Afraid to Leave"

Denny's marriage of nine years was a disaster. He was attractive and intelligent and a successful businessman in his thirties. No one understood why he put up with his wife's verbal and financial abuse. He kept secret that she refused to have sex with him. She went out with other men on thinly disguised dates, laughing when he acted jealous. She pushed it so far as to have another man in their home, and Denny walked in on them. He finally demanded a divorce.

She refused to leave "her" home, and Denny had to move out. He lost twenty pounds after six weeks away from his wife and was on three antianxiety medications that failed to help him sleep. She refused to give him a divorce and said he was exaggerating the problem. They didn't need therapy and could work things out "like we always have." He was tempted to return to end the agony of separation, although he knew it would be a total betrayal of himself. He'd left her once before, two years into their marriage, after she'd had a flagrant affair. He promised himself that he wouldn't go back this time, but that promise was wearing thin.

Denny's doctor told him he would be hospitalized if he couldn't sleep and eat. This was the incentive for his very first psychotherapy session. He couldn't explain the compulsion to cling to his wife or why he couldn't bring himself to go to a divorce attorney. His friends and doctor gave him constant support to stay away. "She's poison," they said.

The therapist asked in the session what he feared would happen if he really left her. Denny began to cry for the first time since the separation. Doubled in pain, he wailed, "I'm going to die." His exclamation evoked this memory: "I can feel my stomach in a knot, and my mouth is so dry. I want to scream and run, but I can't get out of bed. I keep thinking about a door being closed and I'm staring at it. Oh, I'm in the hospital! When I was three, they took out my appendix out. My parents had to leave me overnight, and I was alone in a big room. I thought they were never coming back when they closed the door." The therapist asked the scared little boy what he was afraid of, when he thought they'd left him for good.

"My parents were always so loving, I know they didn't want to leave me. I must have believed I was going to die." Now he could see that his inability to leave was meant to guarantee survival for the Child, no matter what it cost the adult.

It may seem absurd that the fears of a three-year-old could determine how a thirty-five-year-old man should handle a wretched relationship. Yet we all have similar beliefs that were formed by powerful, early events. The mind-body connection is fiercely protective and will not easily let go of life. Denny began to consciously comfort and protect his Child, and this allowed him to let go of his marriage.

Challenging the fear of being alone takes willingness to trust in other people during the first phase of separation. It helps to write about the times that you have survived leaving or being left.

The Child has little recall of the joys that followed escaping a bad situation. The Child focuses on the memory of the pain of early separations. It will help you immensely if you turn to others for support the moment you decide to leave an unhealthy dependency. Lean on friends, family, and trustworthy professionals for the reassurance that you'll survive this hard time. There is no shame in admitting you need assistance to take the steps from abuse to freedom.

Assessing If It's Time to Leave

You both felt the joy of connection when starting out and threw off the shame and limits of past relationships. You showed each other your finest selves as you had endless conversations searching for similarities and positive reflection. You not only adored each other, you felt lovable and worthwhile to yourself.

No relationship can stay for long in this first phase of adoration. You'll need to make room after the initial thrill for returning to a more separate sense of self. The Adult wants time alone, and your Protector starts looking for signs of rejection.

This signals the entry into the second phase, where you begin to explore the deeper parts of the relationship. You start to recognize the impact of your differences and find yourselves in conflict. Old habits reappear. Less time is spent sharing thoughts and ideas, and more time is spent talking about problems. Your individual unhealthy trust patterns from long before you met reassert themselves. This can create disappointments and misunderstandings:

- Tender revelations diminish, and the need for privacy is reasserted.

- The ease of saying no to bad habits is gone, and cravings are back, despite promises.

- Fascination and blind acceptance are replaced by the impulse to blame and assume.

- Fear of rejection shuts down the easy flow of opinions, desire, and playfulness.

- Once-attractive habits and appearances are cause for complaint.

The Benefits from These Cycles

Every meaningful relationship goes through several cycles, and the second phase is a necessary part. A cycle is triggered when there is a felt betrayal. The shock of feeling disconnected provides a chance to ask each other if it's time to let go. A return to honest sharing makes leaving unnecessary. Each cycle is an opportunity to understand more about each other and to resolve healthy conflicts. You form new trust patterns each time, and intimacy deepens.

Your relationship is in serious difficulty if you cling to distrust and assumptions rather than talk things through. Nothing can replace trust as proof of love. You may believe that letting go of the whole relationship is the only available choice when things feel rocky. It isn't. There is a final part of the cycle, and that is when the two of you assess the relationship.

Assessing the Relationship Together

Assessment means that you both examine your feelings and assumptions about each other and the relationship. To your Child selves, looking closely at the pros and cons of staying together will feel almost as scary as leaving. It is essential to go about this in a manner that is fair and respectful. "Five Steps toward Honesty" in chapter 8 gives you a tool that you can use together. You may need to dedicate time and money for couples counseling, self-help books, or personal retreats. The reward can be in the rediscovery of your mutual compassion and understanding. The risk is that you'll find out that you're not equally invested in improving the relationship. This knowledge will help you maintain your integrity, so be kind and caring if you face the pain of separation.

When They Refuse to Talk Things Over

Making any relationship work is a shared responsibility. The root of "relationship" is *relate*, which means to tell. You're enmeshed with someone who is unable to tolerate intimacy if he or she won't talk or admit to a problem. Do any of these statements sound familiar?

- "Things are fine. We get along better than a lot of other couples."

- "I'm doing my best. I'm not good with words like you."

- "I'm not listening to you complain about our friendship. You're just selfish."

- "Therapy is a waste. You just want someone to take your side."

- "I'm sick of listening to your whining about feelings. You're crazy, not me."

- "Talking only makes us fight. Let's just have more sex, vacations, or fun."

When someone refuses to talk, tells you that the problems are all your fault, or becomes angry when you ask for closeness, stop asking. Walk away for a specified time. The relationship may be beyond saving if he or she doesn't want to resolve painful issues. This is especially true when you see that the other person doesn't want to support your needs and hear your feelings.

Separation Can Help in Assessment

Sometimes separating is the only way to see what's not working in a relationship. The other person may be as scared as you have been, perhaps even more so, since you're the one who's reading this book and asking yourself these hard questions.

A well-crafted separation agreement can bring both parties to a greater awareness of what to work on. Living apart will help you learn what you want individually as well as together. It's often the only way to escape enmeshment.

The Joy after Leaving

After you finally decide to trust yourself to survive being alone, you will experience a reawakening of your true self. One story of a reawakening is told in a letter from Serafina. She had tried everything she could to reconnect with her husband.

Serafina had been married to George for ten years and had adapted to his depression and dependence. George often told her that he loved her, but he was critical and sullen much of the time. Serafina's friends asked why she stayed and her reply was, "We're soul mates, and we'll work it out." When she had a miscarriage, George refused do the housework or physically care for her as she recovered. He grew impatient when she was cried, and questioned why she was grieving. That awoke her Adult to the fact that he didn't understand her or want to care for her the way she did for him.

George ignored her requests to talk. He said she was crazy and needy. Serafina went into therapy and worked hard on her own guilt and fears of abandonment. She recognized that for years she hadn't really trusted George. She gave him a choice of talking honestly or leaving. Here is her letter to a best friend:

> *George finally moved out on Thursday. He came by and was critical of our wonderful supportive friends and family, said I looked bad, and wasn't interested in hearing about my new job. It was awful. I didn't engage him in talk, just carried a few things out to his car and wished him well. I was emotionally exhausted and deflated when he drove away, but also more clear than I've been in months! This is the man I had been living with, denying the damage it had on my self-trust. I was buried under his fearful negativity. I carefully created a defense against it, which was to shut down. I was grateful for seeing this and felt sad for him.*
>
> *Yesterday I moved our wedding photos to the table of pictures of my friends and family. They fit there, with those whom I love.*
>
> *Last night I had dinner with friends. We played Pictionary and laughed so much and so hard, we were rolling on the floor. I went to bed giggling. I never thought I could feel this lightness and joy again. I realized that living with George was killing my life force, and my love and care could not help us. This is so big. I'm alive. I've made it.*

When Trust Is No Longer an Option

Trust can be destroyed no matter how much you love someone. You lose trust each day if you are in a situation where you are frequently lied to, betrayed, or taken for granted. Asking for what you want is a courageous act. People who will not listen or respond to your request are not trustworthy. Two serious categories make trust no longer an option, addiction, and violence.

Addictions Destroy Trust

Chemical dependency and other addictions are perhaps the most common and lethal barriers to trust. Honest dialogue is impossible. Part of the cycle of addiction is lying and hiding true feelings. Addicts have to minimize the problem to themselves. Denial controls the relationship.

If you care about people whose addictions or compulsions are breaking all connection with you, their children, and life-enhancing activities, don't wait for them to admit they have a problem. It is a loving gift to say you will separate unless they seek help. Leave if they don't get support and guidance. This courageous act of trust is the only one that can give back meaningful lives to both of you.

Abuse and Violence

You are responsible to ensure your own emotional and physical survival. Saying you trust someone who consistently hurts you, even if they claim to be sorry later, is a betrayal of yourself. If you are terrified of being alone, your Child's fears may be so strong that you put up with abuse rather than leave. It's too difficult to address the fears of abandonment by yourself. Connect with someone who understands and will walk with you down the road to liberty.

Contact an agency or counselor who specializes in domestic violence immediately if physical, financial, sexual, or verbal abuse is repeated. Even if you haven't been physically abused but have been violated or hurt in other ways, their services are right for you.

Preparing for the Next Chapter

By now, you have gained self-awareness about how your Child, Protector, and Adult vie for control of whom, how, and when to trust. You have learned that the reactions of the Child are always worth your attention. They provide essential information for quickly identifying and changing unhealthy trust patterns.

In chapter 10 you'll be introduced to ways to increase intimacy with yourself and open to new dreams and possibilities.

CHAPTER 10

Trusting Yourself
More Each Day

My past doesn't control my future!

No matter how many betrayals you have suffered or have committed yourself, you can refuse to let them limit your potential. Turn the hurts from past betrayals into lessons, and make the decision to trust yourself.

Julia Cameron describes the rewards from increasing self-trust: "When we trust ourselves, we become more humble and more daring. When we trust ourselves, we move surely. There is no unnecessary strain in our grasp as we reach out to meet life. There is no snatching at people and events, trying to force them to give us what we think we want. We become what we are meant to be. It is that simple. We become what we are, and we do it by being who we are, not who we strive to be" (2004, 112).

Believing in yourself means opening to your inner wisdom and giving tenderness to the Child. You have learned the hardest truth in the healing of trust: security and self-love don't result from other people loving you or being reliable.

Self-trust is based on self-reliance. When you strengthen your Adult, you can dare to seek intimacy with another. The confidence you need to survive a rejection grows with every promise you keep with yourself and every time you overcome a self-betrayal.

In Sofia Coppola's film *Lost in Translation* (2003), one character says, "The more you know who you are and what you want, the less you let things upset you." Finding out who you really are increases your courage to trust.

Increasing Self-Reliance

The exercises in the first nine chapters asked you to explore your feelings and acknowledge your needs along with your fears. You'll have the opportunity in this last chapter to answer questions about where you want to increase your self-reliance. It's also the time to apply your skills in reaching out to include those you want to trust. You'll reflect on what you've learned and have already changed about unhealthy patterns of trust.

Moving forward and deepening trust with yourself requires that you

- become more trustworthy in your associations with others

- invite healthy and supportive relationships and reduce your dependence on associations that don't support you

- nurture yourself by acknowledging what you want to improve while loving yourself as you are

Becoming Trustworthy

It is more important to be trusted for years than to be liked for a few minutes. Your Child self focuses on trusting others. Your Adult needs to work on becoming trustworthy and maintaining a balance among the three types of trust.

It's hard to deny the panicked cry of the Child who fears disappointing others and is always seeking acceptance. Responding to the Child's fears supports the habits of making assumptions and hiding your truth. The Adult must gently insist on taking the wiser path of compassionate honesty. This will result in developing habits for a healthy trust pattern and will increase your faith in coping with the uncertainty of life and all your relationships.

Habits That Build Trust with Yourself and Others

Healthy habits are built by frequent, conscious practice. The following behaviors will heal the small cracks in trust and intimacy in your relationships, especially with yourself. As you practice these behaviors, your self-love and self-confidence will grow. Imagine how wonderful it would be to be part of a work scene, friendship, and family who are committed to these behaviors:

Speak with compassionate honesty. Wait until you can speak with the authentic voice of your Adult self. Remember that everyone is confused and suffering at times. Don't lie or speak harshly about yourself any more than you would of someone else.

Express gratitude and courtesy to everyone. Never trust someone who is deliberately rude to a child, partner, or waiter. Say "please, thank you, nice to see you, excuse me" to those you love as much as you do to strangers.

Make promises only if you intend to keep them. A casual remark can be taken as a promise. Consider it a compliment when someone takes you at your word.

Put the people you love ahead of others. Ignore the telephone and turn off the television if you have a chance at real conversation. Write down friends' birthdays in your calendar. Initiate loving exchanges.

Say "I'm sorry" and mean it every time you hurt someone's feelings. Apologize even if the betrayal was unintentional. "But I never intended to be critical" shows no compassion and compounds the hurt. Minimizing or shifting blame destroys trust more than the original mistake does.

Clear up assumptions immediately. Assuming what others are thinking erodes trust. Speak directly to and not about others if you are in a conflict. Gossip feeds assumptions. Prepare alone and then invite them to talk.

Make the commitment to lead your life with these habits, and others may want to join in. If they don't, there can still be greater ease between you and other people. You are in charge of the depth of the trust you want to offer. If you are working hard to adopt these habits, and someone else is not, it is kinder to move him or her to a less intimate place in your circles of belonging than insist that they change.

Choosing How Much to Reveal

Many of us pretend to be more trusting of others and confident in ourselves than we actually feel. It's part of our protective coloration to appear confident, regardless of our inner turmoil. Even if we have an abundance of confidence in some areas of our lives, we don't feel it everywhere. People who know us well would be surprised to learn that we have as many doubts as we do. We're quite good at pretending to be in our Adult selves more than we are. This can be a positive quality, unless it stops us from asking for what we want and need from those who trust us to be honest.

You might want to review the "Five Steps toward Honesty" (chapter 8). Revealing your feelings and needs, including fear and hurt, increases the trust and intimacy.

Among my personal heroes are people who spoke honestly of their doubts and failures, then overcame them. For inspiration, read the biographies of the strong and confident people you admire. Mine include Abraham Lincoln, Eleanor Roosevelt, Mahatma Gandhi, Maya Angelou, Buckminster Fuller, Oprah Winfrey, Willie Nelson, and Albert Einstein. All had periods of self-doubt brought on by abuse and humiliation.

What makes these lives worth studying is that these people weren't superheroes. After being betrayed and rejected, they all collapsed. They could not simply brush off tragedy and betrayal any more than you could. What they lost and found again, however, was the courage to trust in themselves. They forgave but didn't pretend to trust who those betrayed them. They redefined relationships in their own circles of belonging. They spoke of finding a greater perspective to support them through their darkest hours and pull them into the light.

Trusting Is Never All or Nothing

Trusting someone is not an all-or-nothing experience. Many of us viewed our parents as the measure of perfection and felt betrayed when we learned that they couldn't be trusted completely. Then we tried having perfect trust in a best friend or first love, telling them our dreams and most embarrassing fears. These relationships were in serious jeopardy if they voiced the slightest disapproval.

This was confusing love with trust, and both love and trust were expected to be perfect. It follows that if someone disappointed us, the trust and love were either gone or never there, which was another profound betrayal.

You have figured out by now that people are not to be universally trusted, nor are relationships to be measured by how long they last. It is the Child's desire to have perfect trust about all things, all the time, in every relationship. To prevent a constant feeling of betrayal, your Adult needs a more moderate expectation of relationships. This means you can love those you can't trust absolutely, but intimacy and belonging are limited.

Each relationship has a different purpose and place in your life. See trust as being segmented into categories to balance your expectations and reduce felt betrayals. Some people can be trusted to show up on time but are irresponsible about money; one person can keep a secret while another would make a better gossip columnist; a deliberate promise is different from a casual "see you later"; and so on, with each area of a relationship.

This also makes the image in your mirror less horrifying. You do not have to get an A+ in every category to be worthy of trust. The next tool can help you assess and appreciate the overall picture of trust you have with another.

Self-Discovery Exercise:
Trust as a Pie Chart

Choose a close relationship where you have a good foundation of trust. List all the areas of mutual interest, along with the characteristics that you value in others, such as "timeliness," "compassion," "responsibility," "being a safe driver," and "similar taste in movies." If this is a lover, include "sex" and "romance" as categories.

Be creative and include many topics from major to minor that reflect your unique relationship. Review the list of habits that build trust from earlier in this chapter and include any that are relevant. Read the whole exercise before beginning. Doing this exercise should take about fifteen minutes.

In your journal:

Draw a six-inch circle and divide it into a pie chart, with as many segments as you have categories, leaving a couple blank for later inspiration. Do the following steps. If you need help, see figure 2 as an example at the end of the exercise.

Step 1. Label each segment with a topic.

Step 2. Measure the trust you feel with this person in each category. Pretend that the center point represents 0 percent and the outer edge is 100 percent. Place a dot inside each pie segment to indicate where your current trust level is about that issue. If he or she forgot your birthday, "thoughtfulness" will be near the center. If he or she borrowed your car and returned it spotless, "responsibility" will have a dot near the outer edge. If he or she is a reckless driver, place the dot in the "being a safe driver" at the center, and so on for each topic. When done, connect the dots to produce a web.

This is a fascinating way to challenge your assumptions. If you keep the chart current in a long-term relationship, you'll see some dots move in and out and others remain stationary.

Step 3. Compare your own trustworthiness on the same chart. Use a different colored pen and rate yourself within each category. Be fair and consider how the other person would rate your driving and helpfulness. This is an exercise in both humility and empathy. Now connect your dots to compare the different aspects.

Step 4. What have you learned about the trustworthiness in this relationship? Are there any issues you want to address after doing this exercise? If so, you might want to revisit the preparation tools in chapter 8. Having a conversation with your "chart mate" can feel scary, but it is a quick way to build trust.

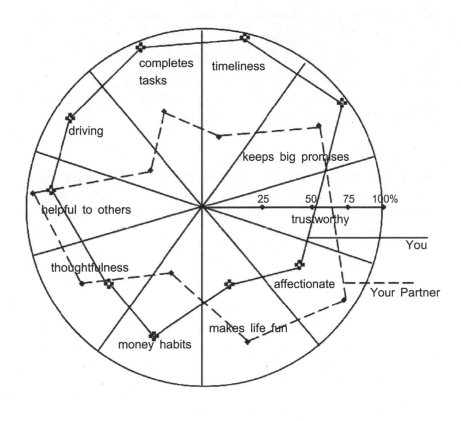

completes tasks
timeliness
driving
keeps big promises
25   50   75   100%
helpful to others
trustworthy
You
thoughtfulness
affectionate
Your Partner
makes life fun
money habits

What Do You Want to Change?

We increase self-confidence when we explore what we want to change about ourselves. Considering positive changes helps us find the enthusiasm our Child lost in ambivalence and uncertainty. Ambivalence dulls desire. We no longer ask ourselves, "What would I do if I took charge of my life?"

Would you consider a new career path, leave or invite a new relationship, or develop a business idea? You might decide to quit an unhealthy habit or begin a new healthy one. Revisit the ideas in chapter 6.

Self-Discovery Exercise:
If You Knew You Couldn't Fail

This exercise encourages you to ask yourself what you want from life. Allow yourself the freedom of the playful Child and brainstorm all the dreams you may have been denying.

In your journal:

Step 1: Take ten minutes to write down the areas where you want to experience success in the next couple of years. Include healing physical problems or addictions, finishing projects around the house, things you'd like to learn, places you want to travel, and big goals you'd like to achieve. Consider these: Lose twenty pounds, quit smoking, write a novel, adopt a child, learn to play the piano, remodel your home, live in Europe for six months, or learn to speak a foreign language.

Step 2. Sort your dreams according to what you want to do first, second, and so on. Use your intuition and imagination. Rewrite your dream list, putting the dreams that call loudest to you at the top.

Step 3. Choose one dream that feels big and important and somewhat daunting and another one that is smaller or more easily accomplished. Recognize your fears as belonging to the Child, feel the Adult's excitement, and listen for the judgment of the Protector. You'll be using these choices in the next exercise.

Inviting the Support You Need

Adding goals to your life is stressful, and you need to find the time and support to devote to them. You can do it all, but not by yourself. You can have it all, but not at the same time. Positive change requires examination of behaviors and situations that keep you too comfortable to be able to reach for your dreams.

Assistance from others along with your own positive energy and sharp focus will accomplish big life changes. Make a place for new plans by reducing the clutter of old goals and "shoulds." You may need to limit contact with people who do not want or know how to support your new choices.

When you start something new, you are in an excited and fragile state of mind. Your Adult hasn't done this new thing before, and your Child fears rejection if you fail. Embrace the habits and people who help you maintain your courage, and cut down on old behaviors and social contacts that slow you down on your new path.

Self-Discovery Exercise: Creating a Magic Circle

The purpose of this exercise is to support your success with a project or area of self-improvement. You can do this by asking specifically for the support you need. This exercise will take about thirty minutes and can be done all at once or in steps.

In your journal:

Draw a circle about six inches in diameter. Write one of the goals from the previous exercise in bold letters at the center. Read the rest of this exercise and look at the model (see figure 3) before you proceed.

Step 1. Write *inside* the circle the names of people already in your life whom you want to ask for support. If you want to learn a new skill, think of anyone in your current circles of belonging who is adept in this area. Include acquaintances you admire. You'll deepen your level of belonging when you invite them to support you.

Step 2. Add categories of people who could serve as inspiration. Write down types of people you want to emulate, such as writers, artists, meditators, nonsmokers, the business-savvy, and so on. Don't worry about where you'll find them. Write down any name that occurs to you, even if you doubt this person has the time to help. Talented and disciplined people often enjoy sharing their passion with those who are serious about learning.

Step 3. Add positive habits and disciplines to the circle that can support your goal. These might include walking, drinking more water, getting up early, or keeping a journal. List the books, classes, or study programs you'll need.

Step 4. On the outside of the circle, list the people, activities, and habits that could distract or discourage you. It may surprise you to see that people whom you love and trust in other ways need to be outside until you are further along. This means seeing less of companions who are not as focused on their own self-improvement. Get rid of the numbing activities that will take time from your goal. Include excesses such as television, junk food, alcohol, or reading every catalog and page in the newspaper.

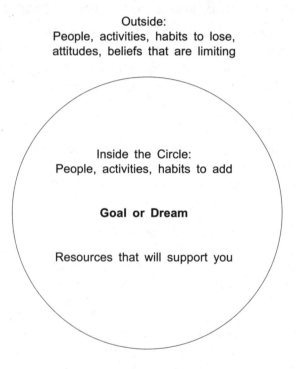

Figure 3: Your Magic Circle

When I decided I was ready to write a book, I didn't tell some close friends and family at first. I imagined them being overly concerned about missing me or that they would worry about me "doing too much." Some, I feared, would question my ability to do this, and I needed no extra help in that regard. I decided to reach out to other writers, asking them for advice and counsel about how to proceed.

I needed to go to bed early, which meant limiting television, casual events, and late-night reading. I woke very early to write while feeling fresh. I added more meditation and exercise to the circle because of the increased stress. I still wanted to keep close contact with friends, so into the circle went "walking lunches" and gym dates. I needed to be obsessed and to have people around who understood and encouraged me to do this hard thing. My life changed. Many of my feared naysayers have turned out to be constant supporters because I was clear and focused. I also met and attracted new people, especially other writers who have become intimates.

I learned that you can't add unlimited people and activities to your life. This exhausts your enthusiasm and encourages failure. Having to "do it all right now, by yourself," harms your chances at growth and is another example of self-betrayal.

Nurturing Yourself

Many of us were taught that taking care of ourselves was more about punishing ourselves into perfection. "I have to take better care of myself" is usually expressed with a sigh while helplessly looking in the mirror.

"Nurturing yourself" should call up a very different image. You might be terrific at nurturing others but have been omitting yourself. How good are you at

- feeding and protecting your family?

- encouraging others to develop their potential?

- giving up your limited spare time for loved ones' happiness?

- paying for treatment for friends because you love them?

How high you are on the list of people whom you consider important and loved enough to be nurtured by you?

Becoming Your Own Best Friend

Eleanor Roosevelt believed in self-nurturing. She wrote, "Friendship with oneself is all important, because without it one cannot be friends with anyone else in the world." A terrific way to increase trust with yourself is to put your name first on the list whenever you dare. It is also important to avoid activities that harm you or are the opposite of nurturing.

What would you think of someone who prevented friends from feeding themselves well, spending time developing their talents, or denying their healthy pleasures and self-care?

Imagine that an old friend comes to stay with you for a few months. She takes total control of your life, choosing your daily behaviors, arranging your schedule, and reordering your priorities. To keep her happy, you

- overeat with her, bingeing on sweets and avoiding vegetables

- keep the television on "for company," constantly surfing for the least awful show

- avoid the little tasks that could keep you organized, like putting things away

- skip daily disciplines, like writing in a journal and exercising because they are boring

- never buy flowers or clean the house except for company

- spend your money without a plan, because she says saving a little each week is pointless

- sacrifice your big life goals so you can take care of other people first

- settle for a life of routine and sigh a lot

Find out the kind of friend you are to yourself with the following questionnaire.

Self-Discovery Questionnaire:
How Do You Rate as Your Own Friend?

Grade yourself from A to F on your performance as a friend to yourself:

_____ *I honor personal resolutions as I would a promise to a friend.*

_____ *I wouldn't delay important plans for the convenience of others.*

_____ *I check my health and emotional well-being often, making changes to improve them.*

_____ *When I make an honest mistake, I tell myself, "No one is perfect, I'll learn from this."*

_____ *I actively seek solutions for problems and pay for the resources to help me solve them.*

_____ *I speak as supportively and kindly to myself as I do to those I love.*

_____ *I anticipate and take care of my special needs when I'm faced with big tasks.*

_____ *I'm as careful about my money as I would be with a friend's.*

_____ *I look for ways to express my creativity.*

_____ *I schedule small steps in big tasks and don't procrastinate.*

_____ *I seek help if I am emotionally or physically in pain and without unnecessary delay.*

Scoring: This is completely subjective. The grades are clues to where you might want to focus on becoming a better friend to yourself.

Your Self-Reliance Frees Others

Being compassionate doesn't mean limiting yourself because your partner, family, or boss can't keep up with your dreams and goals. Claiming your authentic self will free you from the old idea that love is proven by constant self-sacrifice. In fact, your ability to help others greatly improves when you detach from their limits and work on loving and trusting yourself.

As Marianne Williamson puts it in *A Return to Love,*

> Our deepest fear is not that we are inadequate. Our deepest fear is that we are powerful beyond measure. It is our light, not our darkness, that most frightens us. We ask ourselves, Who am I to be brilliant, gorgeous, talented, fabulous? Actually, who are you *not* to be? You are a child of God. Your playing small does not serve the world. There is nothing enlightened about shrinking so that other people won't feel insecure around you. We are all meant to shine, as children do. We were born to make manifest the glory of God that is within us. It is not just in some of us; it is in everyone. And as we let our own light shine, we unconsciously give other people permission to do the same. As we are liberated from our own fear, our presence automatically liberates others. (1992, 190–191)

It scares us to think we may leave everyone behind if we reach for the excellence that these lines promise. You encourage others by speaking your truth, asking for what you truly want, and expecting them to be honest in return. This builds the deep and lasting relationships that have room for everyone's success.

The Courage to Go Deeper

You've been on a hero's journey and faced many fears, some of them long buried. You've learned you don't have to make all your desired changes at once, nor do you have to accomplish them alone. Knowing when and how to trust others comes from knowing you can trust yourself. No one should trust other people completely. It is a betrayal to them to expect they'll anticipate your needs and never be selfish or break a promise. Certainty is an illusion. You also need to cultivate faith as an antidote to your old stories of being flawed. Faith comes to you as a reward for trusting in your own experience.

This is a small book, and the tools and stories are presented to help you discover your truth. It has taken you on a journey where you were asked to confront destructive beliefs. This journey has validated the reasons for your fears and helped you untangle the web of lies that made you doubt yourself. Trusting yourself is easier when you *know* that you are strong, worthwhile, smart, brave, and capable of taking care of yourself.

It takes courage to want to trust. Those who have been deeply betrayed may need to work with a therapist or counselor, who is dedicated to building a trusting relationship with you.

The goal of this book has not been to deny the reasons for your fears. They are real and you'll find more as you take on new challenges. Pay attention to your Child's fears and Protector's warnings as you form new relationships, and consider leaving those that haven't passed the test of trust. The goal is to increase your confidence in handling the feelings, doubts, and betrayals that arise every day.

Any relationship worth having must be risked by being honest—including your relationship with yourself. Telling the truth is possible only when you trust your own feelings and perceptions now, in this moment.

Recommended Reading

Anderson, Susan. 2000. *The Journey from Abandonment to Healing*. New York: Berkley Books.

Beattie, Melody. 1990. *The Language of Letting Go*. Center City, Minn.: Hazelden.

Borysenko, Joan. 1990. *Guilt Is the Teacher, Love Is the Lesson*. New York: Warner Books.

Brown, Nina. 2003. *Loving the Self-Absorbed: How to Create a More Satisfying Relationship with a Narcissistic Partner*. Oakland, Calif.: New Harbinger Publications.

Carmin, Cheryl N., with Teresa Flynn, Barbara G. Markway, and Alec Pollard. 1992. *Dying of Embarrassment: Help for Social Anxiety and Phobia*. Oakland, Calif.: New Harbinger Publications.

Cooper, Robert K. 2001. *The Other 90 Percent: How to Unlock Your Vast Untapped Potential for Leadership and Life*. New York: Crown Business.

Crum, Thomas. 1987. *The Magic of Conflict: Turning a Life of Work into a Work of Art*. New York: Touchstone.

Evans, Patricia. 1996. *The Verbally Abusive Relationship: How to Recognize It and How to Respond*. 2d. edition. Avon, Mass.: Adams Media Corporation.

Ford, Debbie. 2002. *The Secret of the Shadow: The Power of Owning Your Whole Story*. San Francisco: HarperSanFrancisco.

Gorski, Terrence T. 1993. *Addictive Relationships: Why Love Goes Wrong in Recovery.* Independence, Mo.: Herald House/Independent Press.

Hendricks, Gay, and Kathlyn Hendricks. 1992. *Conscious Loving: The Journey to Co-commitment.* New York: Bantam Books.

Hendrix, Harville. 1990. *Getting the Love You Want: A Guide for Couples.* New York: Harper Perennial.

Horn, Sam. 1996. *Tongue Fu! How to Deflect, Disarm, and Defuse Any Verbal Conflict.* New York: St. Martin's Press.

Huber, Cheri. 2001. *There Is Nothing Wrong with You: Going Beyond Self-Hate.* Murphys, Calif.: Keep It Simple Books.

Katie, Byron. 2002. *Loving What Is: Four Questions That Can Change Your Life.* New York: Harmony Books.

Matsakis, Aphrodite. 1998. *Trust after Trauma: A Guide to Relationships for Survivors and Those Who Love Them.* Oakland, Calif.: New Harbinger Publications.

Mellody, Pia, and Lawrence Freundlich. 2003. *The Intimacy Factor: The Ground Rules for Overcoming the Obstacles to Truth, Respect, and Lasting Love.* San Francisco: HarperSanFrancisco.

Psaris, Jett, and Marlena S. Lyons. 2000. *Undefended Love: The Way That You Felt about Yourself When You First Fell in Love Is the Way You Can Feel All the Time.* Oakland, Calif.: New Harbinger Publications.

Thoele, Sue Patton. 2001. *The Courage to Be Yourself: A Woman's Guide to Growing Beyond Emotional Dependence.* 10th anniversary edition. Berkeley, Calif.: Conari Press.

Wall, Cynthia. 2000. *Embracing True Prosperity: Guided Visualizations and Practical Tools for Realizing Your Deepest Dreams.* Audiocassette. Fort Bragg, Calif.: FutureCraft Productions.

References

Brown, Nina. 2001. *Children of the Self-Absorbed: A Grown-Up's Guide to Getting Over Narcissistic Parents.* Oakland, Calif.: New Harbinger Publications.

Cameron, Julia. 2004. *The Sound of Paper: Starting from Scratch.* New York: Tarcher/Penguin.

Coppola, Sofia. 2003. *Lost in Translation.* Film. Los Angeles: Universal Studios.

Covey, Stephen R. 1988. *Seven Basic Habits of Highly Effective People.* Audiocassette seminar. Provo, Utah: The Institute for Principle-Centered Leadership.

Gray, John. 1994. *What You Feel, You Can Heal: A Guide to Enriching Relationships.* San Rafael, Calif.: Heart Publishing Company.

Kirshenbaum, Mira. 1996. *Too Good to Leave, Too Bad to Stay: A Step-by-Step Guide to Help You Decide Whether to Stay In or Get Out of Your Relationship.* New York: Plume/Penguin.

Leider, Emily. 2003. Friends no more. *San Francisco Chronicle Magazine,* September 7, 68.

Mellin, Laurel. 2003. *The Pathway: Follow the Road to Health and Happiness.* New York: Reagan Books.

Palmer, Danielle L. 2003. Spirituality becomes "resilience" and joins the U.S. Army. *Spirituality and Health,* December, 52–59.

Ruiz, Don Miguel. 1997. *The Four Agreements: A Practical Guide to Personal Freedom.* San Rafael, Calif.: Amber-Allen Publishing.

Salzberg, Sharon. 2002. *Faith: Trusting Your Own Deepest Experience.* New York: Riverhead Books.

Seligman, Martin P. 1998. *Learned Optimism: How to Change Your Mind and Your Life.* New York: Free Press.

Wagner, Sascha. 1999. *For You from Sascha.* Lincoln, Nebr.: iUniverse.

Williamson, Marianne. 1992. *A Return to Love: A Reflection on the Principles of "A Course in Miracles."* New York: Harper Collins.

Cynthia Wall, LCSW, earned her master's degree in social work at the University of California, Berkeley, and works in private practice counseling individuals and couples. Her specialty is helping people claim freedom from the limits created by loss and betrayal. She is a volunteer with the American Red Cross and the local hospice in Fort Bragg, CA, where she helps train volunteers and is also involved with the Compassionate Friends, a support group for bereaved parents. A gifted seminar and group leader, she has taught classes in personal growth and self-esteem at the College of the Redwoods in Northern California. Her workshop Trust, Betrayal, and Forgiveness: A Leap of Faith helped her refine the concepts in this book. She has published the ninety-minute audiotape *Embracing True Prosperity* and leads workshops about the psychological and practical aspects of finance. In her latest workshop, The Courage to Trust, she presents powerful techniques that increase self-trust and trustworthiness and teaches how to trust others more wisely. She lives with her husband of twenty-five years, Marshall Rogers, on the Mendocino coast in Northern California. You can contact Cynthia Wall directly at **www.thecouragetotrust.com.**

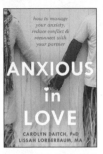

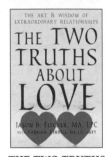

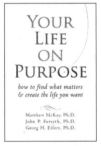